INTERVIEW

MAZE

By

Kevin Mark Eagle

Copyright

ISBN 978-0-578-62500-3 (MOBI)

ISBN 978-0-578-62532-4 (Paperback)

ISBN 978-80-270-3570-0 (Hardcopy)

DEDICATION

I'd like to thank my one and only son, Liam Tobias Eagle, for giving me the fortitude and drive necessary in completing this book on his 6th birthday, February 10, 2018 at nearly the exact minute to when he was born. At 2:22 a.m. in Podoli Hospital in Prague, Czechia on a beautiful snowy Friday morning.

He is my life and inspiration, and I am hopeful one day he will benefit from what has been written in this book, both financially and spiritually in a way of his choosing. Without the grace of God delivering him to me, none of this would have ever been possible. I truly love you with all my heart. Love – Daddy.

ACKNOWLEDGMENT

I'd like to acknowledge "Germancreative" for her hard work on designing and creating the book cover. There were hundreds of images sifted through before finding the perfect fit. It encompasses everything written within the framework of the book. I couldn't be more pleased. I hope it resonates with you as it does with me respective of the journey you're about to embark.

I also want to thank "Sergey Goncharenko" and "Ronan McNabb" for their tremendous dedication in assisting me with the formatting process. In and of itself, it was almost as difficult as the content. Much thought went into the planning of the layout to deliver the best reading experience available.

Lastly, I would like to give my best to the students at Gymnázium Milady Horákové in Prague, Czechia for their support in helping me become a better writer and making this book become a reality. I wish them well in their future endeavors.

PREFACE

Interviewing is much like navigating through a maze. Only "this" maze is no "ordinary" maze! This maze is filled with mystifying twists and unexpected turns, coupled with bewildering obstacles and impediments to cause *confusion* and frustration designed to weed-out the weary and "unprepared."

For this maze will be the ultimate mind game where critical thinking will be paramount in making the right decisions in advancing one's career. Choosing a wrong direction could send you down a pathway littered with landmines – while others may contain booby-traps intended to inflict maximum damage causing one to self-destruct. Life, in it of itself, is much the same.

One wrong (decision) turn can set you on a path of destruction, taking years to recover. Conversely - the interview process is compatible; one wrong answer could spell "doom." This book is *designed* to safeguard you from that by guiding you down the right pathways causing minimum damage.

The candidate who can successfully navigate their way through the maze with the least amount of "self-inflicted" wounds will prove supreme. Taking anything for granted throughout this journey will be one's ultimate demise. By maintaining maximum focus on making the right moves and utilizing the principles in this book, I'm confident you'll be one of the *few* to make it out successfully.

Table Of Contents

INTRODUCTION

20 years of school - now what?!? What will you say when your interviewer looks you in the eye and asks: "Why You?" How will you respond to: "Tell me a time when you had a *problem* and how you solved it?" And this question: "If I were to contact your "friends," what areas would they say you *need* to improve on?" Lastly: "If you had a chance to *change* a decision in your life, what would that be and why?"

Would it be helpful if you had the "correct" answers to the questions above? What if you were provided the "questions" in advance by having an "insider" operating on your behalf? What if you knew every *scenario* before interviewing? Would that be of interest to you? I'm confident it would.

Why? Because, "knowledge" is power, and I'm the *insider* who can provide it. How? By having *documented* every interview scenario and "encounter" traveling through the maze, it enabled me to map-out a safe passageway providing a road-map for your future journeys.

The "Interview Maze" is filled with employer tricks,

maneuvers, deceptions, obstacles, and trap doors that will test the brightest of the brightest. Through this book, I'll uncover these potential *danger* areas and teach you how to "navigate" around them via an *exclusive* look inside interviewing having "personally" conquered the interview maze on multiple occasions." Who am I? An international interview-coach and writer who formerly worked as a Sales and Marketing professional for the following Fortune 100 companies:

√   American Airlines (formerly US Airways) – the world's largest airline.

√   AstraZeneca Pharmaceutical Company – 8th largest pharmaceutical company in the world.

√   AT&T – 9th largest company in the U.S.

√   General Electric – 11th largest company in the world.

√   Grainger Industrial Company – "largest" industrial company in the U.S.

√   Otis Elevator Company – largest people moving company worldwide.

I've had my fair share of interviews. Not one went by where I didn't document every detail leading me in becoming a *master* interviewer within the multi-national ranks. Proper "preparation" – through careful study and crafting "infallible" responses to every interview scenario conceivable, led to a near perfect closure rate.

Sooner or later you'll have to come to terms you must beat out the person sitting across from you in order to secure meaningful work. How will you do that? By being better *prepared* – that's how! And, I'm going to teach you the "how". Whether we like it or not, the world is one large arena on who can *outsell* themselves to the hiring manager. Most everyone will be dressed for success, but which candidate will back it up?

After reading this book – you'll be armed with creating an awesome - sellable CV (resume), have expert knowledge on the "4 – Phases" of the interview process, plus a thorough understanding on how to *master* the dreaded "assessment – center" and competency based interviews (Structured Interview). So grab a cup of power coffee, find a nice resting place (free of distractions) and let's get down to business. The sooner you finish, the sooner you'll be on your way to securing that dream job you've envisioned and deserve. Don't you deserve it? Of course you do. Let's get started!

Chapter 1

COVER LETTERS, CV'S RESUMES

It's no secret that the first million a millionaire will ever make will be their hardest. It is also no secret that the most difficult part to obtaining a well-paying job will be securing the "first" interview. Your gateway in allowing this to happen will be through attaining a personal boarding pass via a well written "cover-letter" - demonstrating your value to an organization. Why it's so important.

A cover letter is a "sales-pitch" on your reasoning as to why you're best suited for the position. This is done through pinpointing skill-sets within the text of the letter connected to your personal work history. In other words - the CV is a "schematic map" of you - whereas the cover letter is a "users-guide" on how to apply that map towards the job.

It should include an engaging question (for starters) to grab the interest of the recruiter - followed by some interesting fact about the company. Owners of companies

4

love to hear how great they are, and how they've taken a company with 2 employees (working out of a garage) to a trillion dollar corporate icon as with Apple.

Therefore, you had better say something of interest about the company in order to keep the recruiter focused on your personal cover letter. For example: 'Your time is limited so don't waste it living someone else's life' – Steve Jobs. Congratulations on launching the new redesigned IPhone X – can't wait!

This quote is one of many by Steve Jobs. No matter whether the recruiter has ever heard this quote before, he or she can see you've taken the time to mention the company founder and are paying your respects. Additionally – a follow up to that is by giving the company a pat on the back for launching the new iPhone. This will help keep the recruiter interested in what "else" you have to say.

Conversely - by showing a general concern about company leadership and their products, it demonstrates you've taken the time to do a little research on the company. The next part will be solely up to you, expressing "why you"? This can be done by providing specific work-related stories identifying key skill-sets necessary for the job in question.

For example: "As a software engineer for the past 12 years developing apps for iPhones with ABC Company – I'm confident my skill sets are a perfect fit for the opening you currently have within your development team. Here's where I can be of help." (Specific story goes here)

The interest of the recruiter will have been gained – providing them reason to continue reading your sales-pitch on "why you?" Companies are out to fill positions of need and will compare your skill sets to other candidates. It's conceivable they could potentially hire more than one candidate; therefore – it's in your best interest to demonstrate how you can be of help. Afterwards - you must drive the point home you are the best fit for their company. How? By offering "explicit" examples of personal work experiences used in tackling difficult challenges.

1st: determine the skills the company is in pursuit of;

2nd: choose a "complement" work experience and wrap it around the "skills in demand";

3rd: show how the work experience (chosen) benefits the company, but keep it to 2 examples, because you'll need to keep some powder dry for the interview.

Additionally, I recommend keeping the letter to no more than "4 paragraphs" with the first paragraph being the "attention-grabber," the 2nd and 3rd containing specific examples, while the last paragraph bringing the cover letter to a close by asking for the interview. Plus, add some strength's about you (in the 4th and final paragraph) as a teaser for what the interviewer might expect to hear about you in the upcoming interview. For example:

√ "To sum up, I'm confident my skills are best suited for this position based on the examples provided above. Moreover, I'm a problem solver and extremely flexible allowing me the ability to work well within your organization, plus I require no hand holding and can start producing results immediately. Thank you for your time, I look forward to demonstrating my skills in person. Best regards, Kevin"

✦ A quick note about this "last" (4th) paragraph; it depends on the job type and situation - but my experience has been to communicate the fact that you are "mature" and require minimum supervision. Companies aren't in the business of losing money, and will like the idea you can hit the ground running without placing a dent in their training budget. Therefore, include that in the last paragraph.

Furthermore, I would add you are "flexible", because corporations love candidates who are flexible. That said, always end by "thanking them for their time", and that you "look forward to a personal interview in order to demonstrate your skills in person." This shows confidence and if they were to pass on you, they may be missing out on a great hire.

In closing - cover letters are designed to articulate how well your skills would mesh within the prospective organization. If lacking in any way, your cover letter and CV will wind up in the trash bin, along with your chances of ever getting an interview (and job). So, don't take this step for granted. Each of which is more important than the next, and the cover letter is no exception!

Therefore, ensure you detail specific job skills related to work situations and how they will translate to future business for the company. Otherwise, you may not be invited for an interview. If you need help with this, to reiterate from earlier, hire a professional. The money you spend (invest) ahead of time, will more than pay for itself upon getting a high-paying job. Besides the cover letter – certify your CV or Resume is up to date and that it best reflects who you are by following my tips in the sections below.

This section is a must read for younger readers and University graduates, plus those with limited work experience; whereas – my veteran readers would be advised to glance over this section in search of enhancements before moving on to Chapter 2 – Interview Preparation & Types.

CV's:

Many ask the difference between a CV and resume. A CV is a *longer* document than a resume, 2-3 pages with a major emphasis on "education" credentials - whereas a resume is used *exclusively* in the U.S. and Canada and is shorter in length, 2-3 pages and mostly consisting of one page. CV (curriculum vitae) is primarily used in Europe, Asia, plus the Middle East, and popular in academia, science, and medical community within the U.S.

Content consists of academic performance – particularly publications written and awards received; professional associations, licenses and teaching experience. Traditional information found on both CV and resumes include: Name and contact information; education; employment history; skills; certifications; foreign languages learned; and (possibly) a summary of your work. Note: There are 3 formats of CV's (Chronological, Functional, and Combination).

This book focuses on Chronological – the *quintessential CV*. Hiring managers and recruiters focus on CV's and resumes written mainly in this format as this is the *gold-standard*. Don't venture outside tradition trying to outthink the unthinkable. Stay within the box and differentiate yourself by writing a *dazzling* cover letter. Hiring managers have plenty of traditional CV's and resumes to choose from, so it's in your best interest to stay within the herd on this. Let's discuss formatting.

All Headings and sub-headings for both CVs and resumes should be *consistent*. Headings should be 18 point font-size in bold and beginning letters should be capitalized. Title or "sub"- heading should have a font size of 14 then 12-point for information "below" the sub-heading. Bullet points for "accomplishments" can be 12-point or lower, but use caution on anything below 10-point Employers will discard anything they deem too difficult to read.

Contact Information:

Write in your first and last name, plus middle name (if you have one). Contact information should include full address – street name and number, city, state or district (if living outside U.S.), country and zip code.

> Note: It's prohibited in the U.S. to ask specifics about personal information such as: age; race; national origin; gender; religion; marital status and sexual orientation; whereas in Europe and surrounding countries – there are more leniencies. Therefore - it's optional for you to include your

age, marital status, race and gender depending on where you reside.

Education:

This is where the major differences lie between a CV and resume. On a CV - Education section should be as detailed as possible - outlining where you attended school and any awards received; publications crediting your research, and thesis or dissertation information. Format: "name of diploma" comes first; followed by "date of certification"; then "name of your University" with dates attended, plus thesis or dissertation on a separate line. Limited experience only? No problem, write in the name of your high school or secondary school with dates attended to the right of the name.

Awards:

Add this section underneath the thesis section (if any). Be very descriptive about the award received and from whom. Often recruiters use "algorithms" in their software to "screen-out" candidates based on specific information on CV's. Awards are definitely popular among hiring managers, so ensure you list them here. Conversely - list any teaching and research experience you may have had with whom and dates. Basically, if any related experience with academia, include it here. Next - employment experience.

Work History:

This will be the most scrutinized section of a CV or resume in determining whether you have the necessary skills to do the job. If you already have the particular experience desired, then companies can immediately put you to work and begin producing revenue versus using training dollars preparing you for the job. What to include: List each job "chronologically" starting with your most recent employer, followed by your first job worked.

One distinctive difference with a CV and resume is that a CV contains most (if not all) of your entire work history vs. only a snapshot with a resume. For those with extensive work histories – a CV would contain most of that while a resume only the last 10 years. Format: Include name of the employer, city location, and dates (14 pt. font size and in "bold"). Plus, directly underneath include your work title then double space; include your responsibilities in 12 point font below that. Afterwards - double space again; include accomplishments and awards utilizing "bullet" points for each entry (12 point or lower). For example:

AstraZeneca Pharmaceutical Company, Orlando, FL 2010-2015

Sales Representative

Responsibilities included: sold various cardiac medicine to cardiologist and internal medicine physicians throughout the Orlando area with a special emphasis on increasing market share.

- Top 10 in Southeast region

- Top 10 in District in total prescriptions

- Chosen to represent Expert panel in SPIN selling techniques

Books – Research:

If you have any experience with writing (professionally or not) you should include this information, even if the job you're applying for doesn't warrant it. You never know if there might be an opportunity within the organization that could use it. Therefore, include any research papers you have worked on here.

Skills:

This section should include any skill sets you have such as: foreign languages; Microsoft Office (basic, advanced, expert); computer skills: coding (HTML, CSS, DRUPAL, JOOMLA); blogging, and any hardware certifications. Anything you deem as a skill should be included here. Note: "Languages" can be listed as a separate heading altogether.

Certifications:

Include any certificates you've received for class work completed, or any professional management courses. For example: "Certified in SPIN Selling Techniques; Dimension Selling; Max Track Selling Techniques; "Train the Trainer" Course; TEFL Certified; Google Ad Words Certified – 2018." Notice I did not *date* "Selling techniques" - but did Google Ad words? That's because Google requires you to update your certificate yearly, or at least every 2 years with continuing education.

Therefore, if you're in a field where Continuing Education is a requirement (as with many professional careers): Drs., Lawyers, Engineers, Pilots, etc. then you should include dates of certifications. Regardless, make sure you include all certifications as this can make or break you when it comes to being shortlisted. The ultimate goal is to *get* the interview. That's the hard part, but once you do, this book will guide you through the remaining steps necessary in becoming shortlisted.

Driver's License (DL):

List your certifications "only" (I.E. Motorcycle, CDL – heavy truck, ECT.). It's not necessary to list your number, nor recommended.

Associations:

If you are a current member of any organizations like: Chambers of Commerce, Toastmasters, or any other professional organizations related to your field, list them here. Social organizations (University) are also welcome in this section. Moreover - there's a plethora of international networking organizations offering memberships. Include those here as well.

Extracurricular Activities:

Europe contains a program called - Erasmus in which students can study abroad for 1 to 2 semesters where the

EU provides funding assistance to help with cost of living expenses and so on. *Include* this experience here as well as other pertinent activities like "volunteering" or being a camp counselor in a summer camp. Employers want *"well-rounded"* individuals who have shown leadership in various roles, so any voluntary work would be highly recommended to include in this section. Now let's discuss resumes.

Resumes

Resumes are generally shorter in length than CV's, but may contain up to 3 pages (general rule – 2 pages max). The focus is more on individual skills and work history than awards and academics. In contrast - resumes do contain performance awards like: President's Club winner, Salesperson of the Year, and Top Revenue producer displayed via bullet-points. They can be tailor-made to suit the specific job you're applying for, whereas a CV is a *"static"* document containing every job worked. Resumes are often *screened* by software using specific "keywords" on demand.

Accordingly, take time and polish up your resume using dynamic language that will allow it to stand out. For many, this is a daunting task, so I advise hiring a professional firm specializing in this service.

The hardest part in getting a job is having your resume *shortlisted* from the many job applicants seeking the same opportunity. The greater the benefits package - the more (resumes) competitive it will be. Once selected for an interview, you'll be in a great position for success utilizing the knowledge contained within this book.

We touched on the various formats with CV's; likewise, the rules for resumes are no different. Chronological (traditional) resumes are by far the "gold-standard" and the *prototypical* resume you should use. Hiring managers want to see employment history with dates worked, followed underneath by job responsibilities in an easily readable format. Using another resume type could land it in the garbage - so beware. Resumes should be tailored to specific jobs and their requirements. This can be accomplished by including specific "keywords" contained in job descriptions in order to gain the attention of recruiters, versus trying to do so with fancy graphics.

Take Google for example, you search by typing specific keywords in the search field and Google does the rest. It's good to keep this in mind when writing text for your resume to satisfy the *robot-search algorithms*. Furthermore having multiple "versions" based on specific "content" is encouraged, as long as the main idea remains the same: company name, job title, location, and dates worked. Speaking of which - *content* in the form of cover letters is a great way of demonstrating skill-sets by expressing personal work-related stories. We'll explore this in heavy detail in the upcoming chapters.

Chapter 2

INTERVIEW PREPARATION & TYPES

As candidates enter into the interview maze many will get lost, panic, and ultimately turn back in search of safety. In contrast, a select few will remain calm and make it through, unscathed. Interviewing involves stages which increasingly become more difficult as to the level of questions as one advances - leaving little wiggle room for error.

In the end, a vast majority of candidates will have run into "dead-ends" - ending their chances of moving on to the next round; while the remainder will likely participate in an "assessment center", or be interviewed by the company's top brass. Either way, you will have navigated successfully through the most difficult parts of the interview process. So before digging into the framework, let's lay some "ground-rules" for properly preparing oneself before entering into this maze full of surprises.

Interview Journal:

Mazes and chess are much alike. To be effective at them,

one must be aware of all possible movements to keep out of harm's way by not repeating the same mistake (movement) twice. The same can be said for interviewing. The more interviews you take on, the more experience gained. In order to master the skill of interviewing, one must learn from making the wrong move, turn, or saying the wrong thing. How will you know? This will be the difficult part, but the short answer is - you really won't until you begin *recording* explicit details of actual interviews. These must be kept (together) in one place called your *"Interview-Journal."*

Before implementing this, I had no idea where my *mishaps* were originating from. I looked the part by dressing well and used ideal body-language (see – Chapter 3). Consequently, I often made it past the telephone interview and into the latter rounds of the Face-to-Face interviews. However – I frequently "erred" in some manner (unknowingly). Then, upon recreating the interview step by step (similar to a crime scene), recording every detail imaginable, I began seeing problematic patterns.

Pertinent details often documented were persons to whom I interviewed with (names & positions); questions asked and my responses. The cue's the interviewer displayed (good or bad) and their reactions to my answers. This was done the minute upon leaving the building to record as much information possible to keep from forgetting critical details, which could be of benefit for future interviews.

Having said that, this journal won't get you hired, but it can help you from making the same mistakes *twice*, decreasing your odds of making a wrong turn and running into a "dead-end." So be sure and document everything. One other hidden reason as to why note-taking is crucial.

Why Interview Journals are Essential:

Today more than ever, securing high paying jobs has become so competitive, that some recruits are willing to do or say anything to get them - including lying! This has occurred at some of the highest levels within the employment ranks including: NCAA Head Coaching positions and Principles of highly sought after schools offering lucrative salaries. How could this be happening in today's world with all the checks-n-balances with technology? The simple answer - *consistency*!

These cons were able to survive by sticking to their story, albeit imaginary. The lesson learned from this is to know your resume (CV) inside and out. They were good liars, but in the end they got caught and were justifiably fired. Therefore, if anyone reading this book is contemplating "stretching" the truth (Full Disclaimer: I do not condone this activity) you had better *"own it"* and be able to back it up with a believable story.

Bottom line – just don't do it! I realize it's a competitive world and at times you have to do what you have to do. But, it would be simpler for you to *qualify* yourself through taking specific courses and through gaining actual work experience. What's the point in lying? It will eventually catch up to you.

Despite this, you will come across "smooth-talkers" and BS-artists known to be full of it. That's part of the game. Occasionally, the storytellers will win, most of the time they'll lose having been exposed for who they really are. The take away message is to have your story ("pitch") *down*. Then, if asked about a particular situation concerning your resume (CV) you'll have no difficulties in answering it. Let's turn our attention to the types of interviews you may encounter.

Interview Types:

- o Telephone

- o Panel

- o Group

- o Skype

- o Face-to-Face

Preparation for a phone interview should be the same as with a face-to-face interview. Though it will not be as intense as being in front of a hiring manager, there are potential *landmines* one could encounter in choosing a wrong pathway. Therefore, it's important to know your "pitch," your "story" if you will, and to have it down pat. More importantly – one must be wary of any employment gaps or problem areas within their resume. Rest assured, an experienced recruiter will surely ask about these red-flags in the event they exist.

Keys to a Good Phone Interview:

Voice "*reflection*" is the single most important factor in a phone interview. Put it to work for you. Getting a new job is an exciting undertaking. A candidate's voice should reflect that. A candidate's answers are equally important, but if one were to come across as not being interested in the job based on their voice, the interviewer will pick up on that fast. Another suggestion is to dress-up, at least business-casual (tie unnecessary) as it will provide a good professional frame of mind before the call takes place.

Lying on the couch with the TV on and one hand on your smart-phone will set you on a crash course for disaster, making the selection process that much easier for the hiring manager. Interviewing is serious business, treat it as such. Have your resume in front of you and make sure you review it one last time before the call. Also, keep a pen close by with a blank sheet of paper for writing down notes. I would refrain from typing on your computer, because nowadays smartphones can pick up the slightest of sounds. The last thing the interviewer wants to hear are your hands tapping on the keyboard.

Conversely - punctuality is extremely important. Be at your desk at least 15 minutes before, and absolutely no later than 10 minutes before the scheduled call time. It's possible that you could receive a call earlier due to a cancellation, so it's best to be on guard in case that were to occur. Upon accepting the call, have pen and pad ready and immediately write down the interviewer's name. If I had to attribute one thing to my interview success, it's the fact that I always found "common ground" with my interviewer.

So, if at any time someone tells you to call them by first name, take it as a golden opportunity to build rapport and don't waste it. The more you apply it, the increased likelihood that your interviewer will become more comfortable with you. Surprisingly, phone interviews screen out 80% of the field. Voice reflection and enthusiasm are critical factors when it comes to this screening process. Therefore, it's essential in articulating answers in a meaningful manner in order to get a fair shake.

Don't make a wrong decision by going out the night before, getting soused, and smoking a pack of cigarettes. Your voice will indicate as such; setting you up in being crossed off the list - before you know it. Instead, get plenty of sleep and act like you want the job or else you won't *get* the job. I tell my clients repeatedly – *"Show up, don't throw up."!* These are very important words to live by. Live by that motto and success will come your way.

26

Ice-Breakers & Real-Life Phone Examples:

The interviewer will likely begin by asking some ice-breakers before verbalizing the most popular interview question: *"Tell me about yourself?"* This will be covered in massive detail during Phase – I Introduction (Chapter 5). For now, we'll cover the fundamentals. An example of some of the ice-breaker questions could be: "How are you today?" Or, "What are your thoughts about this job opportunity?" Upon answering, you should do so in a way that demonstrates enthusiasm for being selected for the interview. Having said that, be prepared to answer would-be follow-up questions as to "why" or "how" regarding each of your personal responses. Let's take a look at a sample call:

I: Interviewer | C: Candidate

I: "Hello Kevin, how are you this morning?"

C: "I'm great! Thank you for asking, and you?"

I: "Doing well, thanks. What are your thoughts this concerning opportunity?"

C: "I'm very excited to have been chosen to this interview for position."

!Warning! – potential "landmine" approaching.

I: "Is that so? Tell me why."

C: "Sure, I'd be glad to. I use a vast majority of your products and would be honored to represent your brand as I'm confident I could sell a ton of it given my knowledge."

I: "Oh, that's great to hear, ok then, let's continue by you "telling me a bit about yourself."

At this juncture – you *avoided* what could have been your undoing within the first 5 minutes of a telephone interview. You'd be surprised at how easy these little *"follow-up"* questions can "sink" a candidate. The important point is to know in advance how to answer "Why" follow-up questions for *every* response out of your mouth. This will "vastly" improve your interview skills. Many lose site within the maze by getting blind-sided with unexpected follow-up questions; having no clear direction on where to go or how to answer them. Don't be a victim of this. Be prepared!

In contrast - it's astounding to see the change in attitude from the interviewer after being offered the job. I've had some real ego-maniacs who treated the interview as an interrogation, then afterwards, acted like my best friend. They would often boast having just put me through the grinder; explaining how they felt they "had" me, after grilling me throughout the more challenging phases of the interview.

Luckily, by having my interview journal and planning in advance helped me overcome these overzealous managers. So be on guard at all times, even just for an ice-breaker question leading off the interview. After the ice-breakers and pleasantries have been established, questions about your last job (or two) worked will likely be asked. Be prepared to answer in depth about your responsibilities and accomplishments. In Chapter 7, we'll cover the *S.T.A.R. Technique* extensively, which will help you with this.

That said, one question sure to be asked by your interviewer is: "Why did you leave your previous job?" And not having a plausible reply will guarantee an early departure. Navigating through the interview maze will challenge the most skilled "critical-thinkers" in choosing the right direction. The question above is where one could easily venture off path never finding their way back - leading to an early dismissal. Play it safe and stick with the following response that has stood the test of time:

√ "A better opportunity presented itself and I took advantage to advance my career."

Otherwise, giving too much information belaboring a point on why you switched jobs could land you in the "danger zone." No one can fault you for seeking better opportunities – including the interviewer. The statement above leaves no openings for "uncovering a problem." If asked a follow-up question to explain in more detail simply say:

√ "You reached your maximum potential with your last employer and it was time to advance your career in a more meaningful way"

Play the interviewer's game by giving them the exact same answer, but in a different way. They will move on when they see there isn't anything to be gained (negatively) by your answers. Ultimately - the phone interview will last (in most cases) 30 minutes and will usually end by the interviewer asking if you have any questions. There's a common cliché, but an important one to keep mind of: *"Always be closing"* - or simply, *"A-B-C."* It sounds simple enough, but when given the chance it's important to know where you "stand" in terms of advancing to the next round. So when asked if you have any questions for the interviewer, "seize" this opportunity by asking the *"Money Question!"* What's the money question? Read on.

$ "Based on my interview with you today, is there any reason keeping you from advancing me to the next round?"

This single question has offered me lifelines where the interviewer had already given up on me. Before I receive all kinds of hate mail - for fear of making an enemy out of the interviewer - you have to know where you stand or else you can kiss the job goodbye. If you don't ask - you "won't" receive.

The question above is only a suggestion and fits within the framework of the information you're trying to obtain. That is, whether or not you're moving on and why! If not – "tell me 'why' so I can fix it"! *If you don't ask why, you cannot fix it.* It's all in the manner how you ask (word) the question.

I've given several suggestions below asking the exact same question, but in different variations interjecting a softer tone. The fact remains that you still need to ask it. Why? To give yourself a (second) chance to stay in the game in the event the interviewer has decided to pass on you. You won't know if they have unless you ask. By asking, you can overcome a potential objection the interviewer has of you in moving you forward. For example:

Let's say that the interviewer really likes you, but you lack experience the other candidates have. Honestly, hiring you will be risky, but by asking the "money-question" (introduced above) the interviewer could respond in this manner:

- "Lucy, today your interview was solid, but you're just a little short on experience compared with the other candidates. However, in the future we'll keep you in mind for any openings that come up."

Bam! You've just discovered two very important pieces of information. One, they aren't going to advance you, and the second being the reason "why"! Had you not asked the question, you would have been sent home without having known why. Now you have the opportunity to use your charm by selling the interviewer as to why you, potentially saving yourself, while bumping another candidate in the process. For instance:

√ "Thank you for the input. Please allow me to address your concerns, though the other candidates may have more experience than I; I assure you they don't have the drive and passion I do; in fact – upon taking over my territory, it was the worst performing territory nationally, and within 12 months I turned that around. This was accomplished by problem solving and working day and night (including weekends) to give my customers the service they deserve. This led to me receiving "employee of the month" for 6 consecutive months. If given the chance within your company, I could duplicate these efforts."

Now I could go on, but you get the point. Clearly, if I were in the interviewer's position, I would find a place for Lucy. Any candidate who's willing to fight like that for a job deserves a position in my book. One more thing - companies want to hire candidates who are "*hungry*." There is no substitute for hungry employees. The person who can clearly demonstrate that (above all others) will be hired. Below are examples of the money-question reworded in a way that lends a softer tone:

√ "Do you see any concerns or pitfalls from our conversation today that would keep me back from moving on to the next round?"

√ "May I ask, are there any areas of concerns I should be worried about going into the next phase of the process? 'Not at this time.' Great! When should I expect a call regarding the second round?"

√ "Based on your experience as a hiring manager, do you have any suggestions I could work on in order to fully prepare myself for the next round?" Follow that up with: "May I ask, is it safe to say I will be invited to the next round based on our conversation today?"

√ "Based on all the research I've done thus far and after speaking with you, I'm confident this position is the perfect fit for me. Could you suggest any areas I may be lacking that'd hinder me from moving on to the next round?"

The objective is to gain information about your status on moving forward to the next round. The questions above will aid you in facilitating this process. I consider this one question (worded in a "non-confrontational" way) to be the mother of all questions when interviewing – which is why I call it the "money question," because if you don't ask it, it could cost you the job, hence money.

You will be amazed at how effective this line of questioning is. Many other candidates will wind up spinning around in circles asking insignificant questions about job benefits, pay, and other useless questions. Don't go there!

Ask the one "money" question above, wait for the "objection" and answer it. If no objections appear, you'll advance. I can think of no instance where this did not hold true for me. No objections meant I advanced, period! On the other hand, if objections do arise, one may have (unknowingly) chosen a wrong path inside the maze. Nonetheless - by having asked the question in a non-confrontational manner, one can potentially redeem themselves setting up a pathway for being shortlisted

35

among the final group. The 3 objections you'll likely uncover upon asking the money-question:

1) Lack of Experience

2) Gap in Resume

3) Lack of Education

Having pre-planned "*scripts*" for each objection is highly recommended. Without them, the chances are great a candidate could unravel in the heat of the moment searching for a suitable answer. For that reason – it's imperative to prepare beforehand in case an objection presents itself.

If so, you'll be ready to answer without hesitation. Thus, upon asking the money question, listen intensely to the interviewer's response. If no objections appear, then it's likely you will move on. In the event you don't, know in your mind there's nothing more you could have done.

A large portion of Chapter 8 (Selling Yourself & Overcoming Objections) has been devoted to this. To sum up the phone interview, get plenty of rest the night before, be ready for the call 10-15 minutes prior, and have a copy of your resume prepared. Upon taking the call, jot down the interviewer's name and be ready to answer, *"Tell me about yourself"* – then expect to speak about your latest work history, including why you left each job.

Speak confidently and clearly and be aware of potential landmines after being asked *"follow-up"* questions regarding personal accomplishments. More importantly, ask the *"money"* question at the end of the interview, wait for objections and answer accordingly. Panel interviews are next.

Panel Interviews

Panel interviews consist of "two" or more interviewers in the same room with at least "one" or more candidates; whereas "Group" interviews contain one or more interviewers with "more" than one candidate in the same room. Due to time constraints, more companies are increasing their use of this interview type. The structure is pretty simple.

Taking would-be individual (one-on-one) interviews and combining them into *one* big interview session with various department managers. Besides better "efficiency" - another *productive* measure is the ability to compare notes "instantaneously" after each candidate is interviewed, allowing for quicker decision making. Therefore, it would behoove a candidate to try and obtain the company personnel conducting the interviews beforehand, in order to prepare a few targeted questions for each.

The possibilities could stem from the Marketing Manager, Sales Manager, HR Manager, Project Manager, IT Manager, or even possibly another manager depending on the job position in question. The "approach" to this interview type will be a tad different than with an individual face-to-face meeting.

For instance, building rapport and a common interest with managers conducting the interviews will be more difficult. This is due in part to the interview questions coming at you from multiple directions (managers) within the same room. The other part being that it will lead to further follow-up questions based on other managers' questions leaving very little time for rapport building.

The reason for this type of interview is that it allows hiring managers the ability to see who can best *think on their feet.* How should one handle this type of situation? Just treat each interviewer as you would an individual

38

interview and calmly listen keenly to what's being asked of you, then respond.

Important Side Notes:

Upon entering the room, introduce yourself to each manager utilizing proper "eye-contact" and ask for their business card for the purposes of following up later. Regarding the actual interview – it's vitally important to *involve* everyone in the room.

For example, let's say you're faced with a panel consisting of 3 interviewers sitting side-by-side. A question is asked from the far left seat (seat - 1). Simultaneously while answering, a follow-up question appears from the far right (seat - 3). What's protocol in a situation such as this?

Address the interviewer's second question by shifting your body slightly right, making eye contact and kindly say you will answer them in just a moment. Then slowly shift back left, finish responding to the original question. Meanwhile, it would be advantageous to involve the manager in the middle (seat - 2) by quickly glancing in their eyes as you shift back left. Finally - refocus your efforts back on the original manager (seat - 1).

This approach will demonstrate your professionalism by involving and "acknowledging" all panel members, not just the one directing the question at you. Treat the panel-interview as a *major* opportunity. Why? Because you, along with 3 other managers, will be in the same room together for 60 minutes offering a chance for you to demonstrate your capabilities. Despite the fact you may only be applying for a sales position, the company potentially could be in the middle of an aggressive expansion, which may result in the need for hiring future managers.

This means the company will be on the look-out for talented prospects that can *fast-track* their way into the management program. So never underestimate an interview regarding potential value to your future career. Let's now have a look at the Group Interview.

Group Interview

Group interviews are similar to panel interviews with one key difference; more than one candidate will be present. They can either be announced or unannounced. If you're invited and discover a group interview will ensue, remain calm as the other candidates will be just as surprised and nervous. Why companies use them? To see how well you work within a group setting and for economic reasons.

For instance – let's imagine a company is in need of a replacement after losing a key member of a project team. If a replacement isn't hired soon, many projects will be delayed. Consequently, the group interview is a fast and efficient way of screening multiple candidates at once. Usually 5 or so candidates will interview within one room with several interviewers. *Three* interview scenarios are genuinely used.

1st: Candidates within the group will be required to answer standard interview questions bounced around the table.

2nd: Candidates may be interviewed individually after the group session.

3rd: The group may be required to complete a group task in determining workability within a group.

Managers will judge candidates' interactions with the others plus the validity of their answers. Key points to consider: First, don't panic upon discovering it will be a group interview. *Get to work!* Immediately begin *"working the room"* – by introducing yourself to the other candidates. Be sure and jot down their names to be used at a later time.

Conversely, do so in a casual, less-overbearing way, but in one where you make the others feel as though you're all in it together. The truth of the matter is, you're not in it together; though - the others will be oblivious to this. Doing this will help you feel more at ease upon getting to know everyone. On another note:

Be aware of the fact that the company could be in the market for more than one candidate, so be yourself and let the interview come to you. Second, once you're asked a question by the interviewer during the live session; incorporate the information you recently gained by articulating the other candidates' names into your response like so: "That's a good question! In fact, Lucy and I (girl you met 15 minutes ago) were discussing this *very* question in the hallway. I believe I'm best suited for this job because…"

This will show leadership and the fact you took the initiative to "work the room" beforehand. Finally, *stand out*, but for the right reasons. Being overly aggressive and domineering will turn the interviewers (and those around you) off leading you to a quick exit. Don't be that person. Listen keenly instead. Acknowledge other speakers by nodding your head and chime in when it's appropriate, offering solutions on the topic of discussion.

Final note: In Chapter 9 – The Dreaded Assessment Center, we'll explain the "group activity" in explicit detail, which has many parallels to the group interview. Let's move on to an ever increasingly popular method of interviewing via Skype.

Skype Interviews:

In the digital era of today, managers are working from their home offices more so than in years past. As a consequence, online interviewing, in the form of Skype and others, has become increasingly popular due in part to its cost effectiveness and convenience. In consideration of this progressively new trend, how should one prepare?

Should the same face-to-face interview techniques be used as with an in- person meeting? Good questions, but the only real difference is the fact that your "*audience*" is changing, nothing less nothing more, thus the reason the approach should remain the same. Skype interviews can consist of one or more people in the same room; or can be a group call with a number of managers in attendance from various virtual locations.

Regardless of nature, body language should remain the same as if you were seated in the same room. Naturally, it's an environment to where you may feel more comfortable, but that doesn't give you an excuse to relax. On the contrary, it will be more difficult for you to build rapport. Despite this, it's not a free pass for you not to "try." Do your best to scan the room and find something (anything) to compliment on, otherwise you'll have a hard time separating yourself from the herd.

An example of this could be spotting a designer pen or pencil holder, or possibly even a world famous branded cigar box, such as a *"Montecristo"*. You could then incorporate this finding into a personal family memory. For instance – you could say how it reminds you of your grandfather's office when you were a child.

For me personally, one item I generally look for is a clock. Because of the fact my grandparent's had an old "coo-coo" clock on their living room wall. Each time I hear the sound of one, I'm filled with joy in their remembrance. Now before the actual call keep the following in mind.

The interviewers will have looked over your resume prior and likely will have made a judgment about you based on the content of your resume. Therefore, it's important (when on the call) in finding the slightest little item to complement them on that will change the narrative in your favor. Take for example the Montecristo (cigar) box.

Say you've never smoked a cigar in your life, whereas your father smokes one a day. Maybe the same scenario exists with the interviewer. Though they may have never smoked, the same branded box sits on their desk as a reminder of a close relative.

To add, let's say you mention the cigar box and they express the exact same thought of never having smoked a cigar. If this were to happen – you will have successfully found commonality within your interviewer, setting the stage for them to advance you to the next step of the interview process.

Before the Call:

You would be shocked to hear the number of times candidates fail on a Skype interview, because of a technical glitch within their own computers. Interviewers have only limited time and a plethora of candidates to choose from so don't self- destruct over this. Ensure your connection is working "before" the call. Call a friend to make sure! You can also perform a direct test in Skype by clicking *"test call."*

Most notebooks today have internal cameras and microphones – but too often they conflict with other plug-in software, causing malfunctions. Therefore, it's prudent to check that both the camera and microphone are "on" and working properly. That said – let's now transition to an interview type that gets very little attention, the *"Unplanned"* interview.

Unplanned:

A common theme of being "prepared" will consistently be echoed throughout this book. *Preparation* is the ultimate key to successful interviewing. Without it, unwanted surprises can occur like an "unplanned" interview. An unplanned interview is an unexpected opportunistic situation arising out of desperate need for a company to fill a position. This can be quite common during cycles of low unemployment, which should be music to prospects' ears. Why? Because job requirements normally adhered to by HR are often "eased" by interviewers in order to fill empty positions.

Nevertheless – one cannot bank on this *"rare"* event without having prepared for this in advance. Preparation will require learning how to best express one's self as being the right candidate for the job based on principles in Chapter 8 - *"Selling Yourself."* One word of caution:

Encountering this type of situation will often result in a company wanting you to start *"immediately."* I'm in the camp you should always pay respect to your current (previous) employer by offering them a standard "notice" of your departure. It's not mandatory to provide a notice (in the US) unless written in your employment contract. I gave two weeks (up to one month) for all my employers without being bound by a contractual obligation to do so.

That said, in the EU you are bound by law to provide a specified number of days. In some instances, it's 2 months; incredible as that may sound it's true. The major point is that if a potential employer isn't willing to wait the 60 days for you to work out your notice; you may want to pass on the job. This, of course, if you already have a job, if not, then the situation will benefit the both of you. Let's move on to the most common type of interview you'll undergo.

Face-to-Face Interviews:

Face-to-Face (or in-person) interviews will be the *de facto* encountered for the majority of your career. Mastering them will require a lot of patience, self-study, and real-life experience. Anyone willing to put forth the effort can effectively become a great interviewer. However - one essential ingredient one must possess to have success at interviewing is *"likeability."* The bottom line is - no matter how polished you are and how decorated your resume is, if you're not "likeable" then you'll have a hard time selling the person across from you in becoming their next hire.

However, the good news is, all other candidates, possibly better suited for the job, can be outmaneuvered by demonstrating likeability through *"building rapport"* and by developing "meaningful-connections." We'll cover this in major detail in upcoming chapters. For now, we'll explore how critically important building rapport is to your survival in the next chapter, plus have a look at two of my secret weapons a.k.a. my *"Golden Rules."*

Chapter 3

Rapport Building & Body Language

"Consumer loyalty" is a product of massive advertising efforts (by large corporations) designed to hook you on their prospective brands. Starbucks, NIKE, Coca-Cola, Samsung, and Disney to name a few have tremendous consumer loyalty. It's no secret they have massive advertising budgets built into the price of their products. For them, it's a small expense to pay if they can successfully convert you into a loyal patron. How?

By selling the "perception" their brand is better than the alternative. Once this *"perceived value"* has been successfully positioned in the customer's mind as "their" choice brand, competitors will be *locked out* of this (mental) space, hence producing a loyal consumer. The essence of mastering the ability to interview is precisely the same. By making *connections* and creating *bonds* with the interviewer; one can "lock" out other candidates from this mental space. Upon doing that, your success rate will vastly improve. The big question is: how, and by what method? Let's take a deeper look.

The common denominator responsible for my success was the ability to form a *meaningful* bond with the interviewer. Recall in Chapter 2, the key to interview success is being "likeable." This is absolute *paramount*! In comparison – candidates competing alongside you could be smarter, have more experience and be better suited for the position, despite this; if in this particular situation, it wouldn't mean you would be an *"automatic-out."*

Through use of *"rapport building"* and finding *"commonality"* one can easily turn the tables on these "perceived" stronger candidates. If one were to take one look at me on paper versus the others competing for the same job, it would be difficult to believe I would have had any chance of beating them. However, through the use of my two Golden Rules, it allowed me to level the playing field, which I exploited to my advantage by positioning myself that I was their guy. What are these golden rules? Read on.

Golden Rules:

First golden rule – find *"Commonality"* (same interests)

with your interviewer. Second – *Complimenting.* Complimenting is self-explanatory – whereas discovering "Commonality" is similar to developing a special friendship. The goal in finding commonality is to determine your interviewer's interests and *mesh* them with similar ones of your own. People buy from people they like and can relate to. So finding interests related to yours will help in developing rapport leading to a *meaningful connection.* This will ultimately allow you to *outmaneuver* your competition's strengths: experience and education. In consideration of this - finding common interests will *require* some "effort" unlike complimenting.

For now, we'll focus on how to develop commonality, and then switch gears by sharing tips on how to compliment. Finding common interests is a form of rapport building *quintessential* in developing a bond between you and the interviewer. This is your #1 goal at the beginning of the interview process. Discovering shared interests of your interviewer will put you in the *"friend's-zone"!*

In dating and relationships, these two words are a person's worst nightmare. In contrast - when it comes to interviewing, the sooner you find that zone, the better your chances will be of having a successful interview. But what's the best approach how to accomplish this? By searching for any little "*tidbits*" of information about your interviewer in which you share a common interest. What are "tidbits?" Tidbits are what they sound like, little "bits" or *pieces* of information.

What to Look for:

Let's say the interview is being conducted in the manager's office. What's the goal? Find at least one "tidbit" of information where you can "*link*" it to your life. In other words, uncover a *shared* interest that will provide you a pathway in bonding with the interviewer. Scan everything in the room; from walls; to tables; to furniture; to carpet; to accessories; to any and everything in between.

Look for diplomas; awards on the wall or desks; pictures of any family members (especially children); souvenirs from potential vacation hot-spots you have visited; sports memorabilia such as signed jerseys, balls, hats, bats, footballs and basketballs; anything giving insight as to who the person interviewing you is. Pay particularly close attention to photos.

For instance, let's say you recently took your family to Disney World and happen to notice a family picture taken at Disney World on the interviewer's desk. This is an instant *"ice-breaker"* you can discuss and maybe it will progress into a longer conversation about their kids and yours. People love talking about their kids. So upon seeing any photos of them, in sport uniforms or any other recognizable free time activity, ask them about it. Two other examples:

Identifying a diploma on the wall of the University attended by the interviewer can be very useful. In the event it's your alma mater an instant bond will be established. If different, ask why they chose their specific University as this will open up a nice dialogue leading to some interesting responses. All the same, listen keenly and jot down their answers in your journal. If ever interviewing with them again in the future, this information could be used as an "ice-breaker." Let's move on to my second golden rule – complimenting.

Complimenting:

Do you remember the last time you received a compliment? It put you in a better mood, didn't it? Complimenting is just good for the *soul*. I can't think of anything better in this world than to see people smile. If you can manage to do this with your interviewer, it will increase the odds of you landing in that "friend-zone" we discussed earlier. Let's face it, the office setting sometimes isn't the happiest of places.

Unfortunately, things occurring in people's personal lives can also enter into play during work hours causing potential mood swings. True professionals don't allow these thoughts into their daily work lives, but people are people and mistakes do happen. You don't want to be in that situation where the interviewer is having a bad day, like losing a major account, or maybe having to attend a parent teacher conference due to bad behavior of their child. All of these things can have an effect on how the interview plays out. One way to "reset" the mood is by use of complimenting.

Complimenting is just human nature. It is the simplest of measures candidates can do to improve upon their rapport building skills. You can never go wrong with complimenting except for two points: Never compliment on someone's *appearance* during the *first interview* (unless they mention it first). The other, don't go *overboard!* Interviewers will be quick to notice if you're complimenting too much, and if that were to happen, it would appear unnatural and construe you as trying too hard.

Generally, one to two to start off, then add another during the interview and one more at the end. As you build up interview experience, you'll get a feel for when to use it and when not to. The conversation will usually flow in a direction where it's evident when to use them. It would also be beneficial to end the interview with a compliment while shaking the person's hand. Then, upon seeing that person again, recall what you said to them, and "touch" on it. This will reflect wisely on the fact that you remained focused on them even though the interview had already concluded. By using this tactic you could very easily replace a candidate higher on the list. What are some areas you should focus on when complimenting?

Things to Compliment:

Complement their office building; the cleanliness of the building; how nice the staff is; how organized everything looks; how happy everyone seems. These are the perfect ice-breakers. Other ways to compliment is by mentioning "*milestones*" within a company's history. Companies put employees who *"drink their Kool-Aid"* in a higher light; therefore, it would benefit greatly for a candidate to compliment a company about their history, including their philosophy and ideals. Here's an example of this:

- "Thank you for giving me the opportunity to interview – I'd just like to say how inspirational it is to know how Mr. Jones started this company. I'm incredibly honored to be here."

Some may feel the above statement is a bit *"soft."* On the contrary, being humble is a "good" thing. It demonstrates the company can *"mold"* you their way. It's about making a *connection*, and once you do, it will be difficult for another candidate to break that. Therefore, compliment where appropriate. Mastering the ability to build rapport takes time and requires effort.

There's a plethora of information on the internet you can research, but overall these skills can only be developed by learning the hard way and from experience via actual face-to-face interviews. Another crucial element in interviewing is being able to recognize "body-language."

Body Language & Non-Verbal Communication:

Trivia question. How many seconds does one have to make a good impression? 60, 30, 15, or less? Seriously, what would be your answer? Believe it or not it's "7" seconds! Hard to fathom isn't it? Nevertheless - body language is grossly undervalued as to its significance in interviewing. It's an important facet candidates need to be cognizant of. In discussing the importance of having an interview journal, it's equally important to be critical of one's own body- language shoring up any shortcomings if they exist.

In order to master the art of interviewing, it's critically important in recognizing and reading "cues" while simultaneously reacting to them in an appropriate manner. Some people have a talent for this, whereas others have to work a bit harder at it. Don't fret as I'll cover (in detail) the various aspects of body-language below and provide personal tips on how to respond to the numerous cues associated with them. Lastly, many characteristics of body language go hand-in-hand, so while there may be some overlap in the material to follow, read it all in order to firmly grasp this *intricate* part of the interview process. First up is dress code.

Dress for Success:

Dressing for success is an absolute necessity before you ever step foot into an interview. It demonstrates how serious you are about yourself and your career. Step into the shoes of a hiring manager for a moment. Would you hire a candidate within your organization if they were to show up wearing *shorts* and a *t-shirt?*

The answer for 99% of you would be a resounding "No"! Though there may be an exception out there, let's be honest with ourselves. It's about respect, and if you don't show it by dressing the part then it's likely you won't display it at work. Therefore, *dress to impress.*

Most experts agree upon men's and women's apparel for interviewing. Guys should wear a suit (preferably blue) with a white or light blue shirt and matching tie; whereas girls should where a nice dress that isn't too tight and slightly below the knee line. Being well groomed is equally important. Common sense tells us that being well groomed is a must in today's world of finding meaningful employment. Surprisingly — research shows that sense of smell is regarded as the *#1* factor when finding a mate.

Conversely – it plays a major role in securing a job. Having body-odor is an absolute atomic bomb and job killer. If you want to self-implode, this is a sure fire way of doing so. Furthermore, being cleanly shaven is equally important, especially in *"Hipsterville"* where many are opting to display full beards.

Nonetheless, this trend is here to stay, which fits perfectly in the realm of diversity within a workforce, however facial hair tidiness is crucial in this world of dress-code-correctness. So use common sense, shower beforehand, and apply deodorant; adding a little fragrance is OK too, but don't overdo it.

As a former pharmaceutical rep, I recall my top prescription writer (allergist) who would complain immensely about other reps walking into their "Allergy & Asthma" office wearing a full bottle of fragrance, causing patients to have allergic reactions while sitting in the waiting room. I'm not making this up.

Needless to say, they didn't last very long, because they couldn't read the Dr.'s cues as to why they weren't prescribing their product. It definitely made my job a lot easier. So always put yourself in the shoes of others and pay

59

close attention to your surroundings. A frequent question that often presents itself regarding suit coats for men. To button or not to button, therein lies the question.

Suit Coats:

We've spoken about dress code, so what are the rules for buttoning suit coats? There are 4 button styles (normally) on suit coats: 1 – button (always button); 2 buttons (always button top button); 3 buttons and double breasted suit coats.

Rules for the "double-breasted" suits are simple, always leave buttoned. However, with a 3 button coat, button the middle button, but *never* the bottom one. On the other hand, you "*can*" button the top 2 buttons, but never the bottom button. Now what about while a person is standing?

If you didn't have your coat buttoned while sitting, upon standing, button it according to the rules above. The posture (explained next paragraph) should be straight up with head and chin held high, but not so high that will make you look smug. When stationary, leave your hands at your side, or touch them together by pressing all 5 fingertips together; similar to locking hands for prayer, only that you're not locking hands. Never cross your arms and always maintain good eye- contact explained below.

Posture:

Posture is one form of *non-verbal communication* that is often taken for granted. Don't be a victim of bad posture due to not spending 5 minutes critiquing yourself. Grab a stand-up mirror and take a hard long look at your posture while standing. Or better yet, invite a friend over and have them give you feedback based on posture basics below. There is no excuse in losing a job over posture, period!

This is by far the easiest thing to correct. How? Back up against a wall and practice standing up straight. Touch the back of your head (gently) against the wall ensuring your back is also touching. Hold your head up high, chin straight out and look forward. Practice this while walking around the room in this position. Try not to be too stiff. A slight lean forward is OK, just not to the point where you are drooping or slumping forward like a zombie. What about *sitting* posture?

Posture while sitting is equally important. Ever been to

a party where one person has clearly had too much to drink? You glance over and notice a person leaning over to one side about to fall completely out of their chair. It's pretty easy to see, because they stand out from the crowd. Don't be that guy or girl who stands out by displaying bad posture, whether standing or sitting.

It's important not to "*slouch*" or lean forward in an awkward way. Remember when your mother or teacher would tell you to "sit up straight" as a kid? I remember always wanting to ask – "what do you mean by that"!?! But, that crazy little voice in my head would warn me not to, or else I might get whacked. The same applies in a job interview, only you won't get whacked, at least not physically!

A way to rectify this is to sit up straight; meaning back straight, head held high, and feet parallel to your body shoulder length apart. Upon finding a seat, position yourself slightly forward using 75% of the actual seat without touching the back of the chair. Slightly arch your back and keep your head straight. Extend your arms forward with your elbows and forearms pressed against your thighs. Hold your notebook (containing your resumes) parallel to your feet, and have a copy easily accessible in order to reduce any fumbling.

Furthermore – keep in mind that you may be seated for the duration of an hour or more, so plan on doing this with minimal movement. There's a famous saying, "the one who moves or talks first in a negotiation loses." Don't go there! Sit with confidence and listen to your surroundings picking up any *tidbits* to be used for building rapport later.

Tip: You shouldn't ever feel too comfortable sitting in the chair, hence the reason your back should never touch it. The reasoning is simple. The more comfortable you feel, the easier it is for you to lose concentration, risking making a bad decision. Focus on the objective here in finding "tidbits" of information to help you gain common ground with your interviewer. I cannot stress this enough. Finding common ground will "exponentially" increase your odds of a successful interview and gain you one step closer in obtaining your dream job.

Mirror Approach:

Eyes are the "gateway" to your *soul*. It's impossible to make a connection with your interviewer, or anyone for that matter, without making eye-contact. However, the important thing is to use it appropriately in a manner which won't *turn-off* the interviewer, making them want to run for the exits. Too much eye- contact can potentially cause this.

For example – ever been on a first date and the person repeatedly *stare* at you without taking a breath? How did it make you feel? Probably not something you want to talk about. I concur. We wouldn't want that to happen during an interview either. On the contrary – using the "mirror approach" is something we do fancy during an interview. In fact, I consider it one of the top forms of *"non- verbal"* communications around. What's the mirror approach?

Is it those funky mirrors you see at haunted houses that make you look tall or short; fat or skinny? No, not quite, but those mirrors do create quite a stir, don't they? The mirror approach is a very powerful interview tool that has been a big complement in helping me *land* the majority of my jobs. It consists of *adopting* the same "verbal" and "non-verbal" communication between you and the interviewer.

While there isn't a specific science as to when and where you should use it, given time and experience you'll get a better feel on when and where to do so.

For instance - if the interviewer begins to talk softly you should do the same. If they move their body a certain way, "*consider*" doing the same. Hence - similar to an effect as if they were standing in front of a mirror with you on the opposite side.

One may think this is akin to "mimes" in crowded tourist areas, who make their living off of mimicking "exact" body movements of tourists. It's similar in nature, but the difference lies in that a mime "*copies*" your every movement; whereas - if you were to do the same, you would be escorted out of the building fairly quickly. More examples:

If your interviewer changes positions in their chair to a more comfortable position, you should consider doing the same. Whenever your interviewer makes eye-contact with you, you should definitely do the same. In other words – don't look away as this may be mistaken by the interviewer that you're not interested in the position. Another very important example is to mirror your speech and intonation.

If you're interviewer is talking softly, then you should also speak softly. However – if they are shouting don't mirror this, because it's possible they may have hearing difficulties. Just raise your voice a bit, but not to the point of shouting. Use this technique where appropriate; in contrast – be careful not to fall into the trap of being a "mime" where you copy every move. Let's explore why this technique is vitally important.

If you were to take a close look at your friends, you'd agree you all have something in common, right? Securing a job is not any different than finding a best friend. Good friends are hard to come by. That said - *trustworthiness* is an important characteristic in finding one. The same can be said for the mirror approach. Upon using it – "trust" between you and the interviewer will slowly begin to materialize, thereby creating a meaningful bond. This is the essence of building rapport!

Companies are interested in hiring candidates that are *likeable*, but also people who they can trust. No matter the situation, I always try and put myself in other people's shoes in order to give myself better perspective. The same applies with job interviews. I always try to do what I can to befriend the interviewer. Many times it will give you a leg up. Despite this fact - sometimes the interviewer is just a *cold fish* and there's not much you can do in that situation.

Usually the attitude of the interviewer is indicative of the management style the company employs within their workforce. I always keep that in my mind when I interview with a company. Sometimes by not getting the job, they're actually doing you a favor, which can lead to a better opportunity elsewhere. So if you ever encounter a situation where the interviewer is acting a bit aloof, you're probably better off moving on.

Picking up Cue's:

Improving skills in this area will *exponentially* improve your interview success.

In the literal since, cues are simply signals (verbal or non-verbal) from one person to another to elicit some form of action. In an interview – cues are signals (subconscious reactions) given off by an interviewer in response to a candidate's answer to a previously asked question. These could resemble intricate little body movements telegraphing what a person is thinking. Let's look at some examples. Let's say you're running late for an interview, which by the way should never happen (no excuses); and as you walk in to greet the interviewer, you notice a frown on their face as you shake their hand. This should signal to you that they are not happy and that you have some "work to do."

Now it's obvious that the person may be a little agitated at your tardiness, but if they were to *show* (telegraph) this reaction, then you have a "*lot*" of work to do. The possibility does exist to where you may not be able to recover from this. Despite that – give it all you've got and let the cards fall where they may.

There are hundreds more we can look at and I'll provide a few of them shortly, but let's keep it simple. Just look for cues indicative of "positive" and "negative" body-language. This will allow you to adjust accordingly during a "live" interview situation. Some negative body language can include:

Crossing arms; tapping fingers while speaking; wearing a frown; speaking in a condescending tone; not making eye-contact; giving short responses to your questions; asking no follow-up questions; providing "little" small talk at the beginning of the interview; for example – "how's your day going thus far?"

Positive Body-Language Cues:

Smiling often, nodding one's head up and down to show agreement; asking about your day; asking if you found the location OK; making good eye-contact while you talk; showing a genuine interest in you without rushing through the interview. Why are these things important? Because, it allows you to assess how the interviewer is feeling via their body-language, providing an opportunity for you to "change direction" for the better. For example:

Let's say you're driving down the road and your GPS alerts you to an accident nearby, suggesting you take an alternate route, saving you a headache (and wait time) due to a possible road-closure. Would you take it? More likely than not, you would as it's the sole reason for buying the device in the first place, right? By having purchased the device, it has served as a means for discovering the traffic accident and adjusted for it in "real-time" by offering an alternate driving route.

In the example above, your brain is your GPS and using

it to help pick up little cues will aid you in reading the situation in order to change it for the better. Upon encountering any potential road-blocks, it will "alert" you to change course, managed by making adjustments in "real-time," placing you back on track for success. Having said that, what are some things I look at? Some of them may surprise you. A general list includes:

Cue's I Look at:

Facial reactions; speed of the interviewer's voice; facial reactions to my responses to their questions; the way they walk; how they interact with other staff members (is it direct, or warm and friendly); how often they make eye-contact with me while walking or talking or both; how they handle my resume; is it easily accessible or do they fumble around a messy desk looking for it.

I watch their eye-movement during the interview, is it focused on me or my resume; are they squinting or frowning; are they rocking back-n-forth in their chair while looking at it (which is a good thing as they are envisioning you in that position); or do they just briefly scan it and ask you – "what else you got?" (This is never good, but at least now you are aware of this and can go directly to selling:

"Why You?" (Chapter 8).

Upon the interviewer receiving phone calls (internally), I listen to the tone in their voice, how they greet the caller, how they say good-bye. This could signal if they're in a good mood or not. I also pay close attention to whenever an office- assistant enters the room.

Specifically, I look at how my interviewer communicates with them, and take notice on whether the assistant is nervous or not. This could suggest that the manager is demanding in a way that his employees are on "edge" and that it may be difficult to work for this individual.

◆ Most Important Cue:

> The single most important cue to pick up is recognizing when to "stop" *talking*. The cue for you to do so is when the interviewer stops writing down notes and raises their head to suggest they have documented enough information about you (on the subject matter just discussed) and are ready to continue with the interview. Upon seeing this, bring the conversation to a close as quickly as possible and wait for further instructions.

Otherwise, you'll fall into the category of being a rambler and the interviewer will lose interest in you.

Other Cue's I Look at:

I look to see if the interviewer rubs their nose; do they place their hands underneath their chin and fix it there. This could be a sign they are trying to figure you out, not bad or good, just indifferent at this time. I especially hone in on how they acknowledge my answers. I'm interested in hearing: "Great" – "Super" – "Nice" – "Sounds Great" – "Wow"; additionally, a head-bob up and down is a "huge" bonus. I know 100% I'm on the right track if I hear these acknowledgements.

On the other hand, if I hear: "Hmmm" – "Interesting" – "OKKK"; plus see hands on their face or glasses, I know I have work to do, and they may have already given up on me. So now what? What to make of all this?

Having said all of the above, what am I trying to gather from all this? To put it simply, I'm looking to see if the interviewer's allowing me in their "friend- zone." Or, are they closing me completely out by conveying negative actions through various cues' and body-language? If the latter – then I treat that as I'm not making a connection, therefore I must try a bit harder in creating one. How?

By finding a way to lighten the mood with a *compliment* or something positive to try and change the interviewer's disposition. You never know what they may be going through in their personal life. As a professional, I never allow my personal life to affect my work, but sometimes others find it hard to follow this rule, which at times can cause challenges.

I was in one particular work situation where my manager had opened up to me about her boyfriend's *infidelity* while making joint sales-calls. She was a total wreck! I spent more time playing the role of a psychologist than actually working.

Despite this, I looked at it as somewhat positive as she had deemed me trustworthy, entrusting in me with details concerning her private life. For the record, I had much rather leave that baggage at home. So use this as food for thought whenever you encounter a situation where the interviewer is being a bit abrasive and unwelcoming.

In spite of this, sometimes it will be difficult in making a connection with your interviewer, no matter how hard you try. Similarly as with dating, ever so often it's just not in the cards, for whatever the reason. Likewise, some positions are just not the right fit, so it's best to not fight it and move on. Don't take it personally, these things happen; just focus on getting better with every interview and study up on "reading" your cues.

Lastly - be sure to *document* every detail that occurred during the interview and record them in your journal. This includes all questions asked and your responses. Taking time to do this will help develop your "preparation" skills aiding you in becoming a better interviewer. By sticking with this approach, it will help set you up for a big "pay-day" in the end. Let's continue our journey into the next chapter to where we'll construct the *"face-to-face"* interview.

Chapter 4

FACE TO FACE INTERVIEWS & 4 INTERVIEW PHASES

The goal of this chapter is to begin putting the building blocks together learned from previous chapters to prepare you for safe passage through the maze. For some, this may be as early as tomorrow, while others just may be looking to brush up on their interview skills and in need of some tips going forward. All the same – this chapter will detail the *4 - phases* of interviewing consistently used among a broad range of (interview) formats.

The information presented will benefit the laymen, in addition to candidates with extensive experience under their belt. By following the rules and lessons presented, you'll undoubtedly be ahead of the game upon facing your interviewer. We'll begin by identifying the 4 - phases now, and then in later chapters break down each one in explicit detail providing you a wealth of knowledge to overcome any interview obstacle. Grab and pen and pad and let's get started.

Having a Plan:

Think of the last time you set out in accomplishing something really meaningful. A task you lacked the confidence in completing; nonetheless - one identified as something important for you to achieve. For runners, this could be completing a marathon. For sales professionals, making President's club; first-time homebuyers, purchasing a house; students - learning a foreign language.

In these particular instances, it's likely a "detailed" plan was laid out involving the use of stages or "*phases*" if you will. With that said, achieving a major goal is no easy task.

On the contrary, in fact, less than 1% of people in the world have ever completed a marathon. Hard to believe isn't it, yet it's true! For friends and others who have run them, I take my hat off to you having seen the training regimens leading up to one; based on which, it's now easy to see why only 1% have ever completed running one. To my chagrin, each of them began 6-months in advance. Why my surprise?

I presumed a lot less effort would be involved. One friend showed me a spreadsheet of the various *phases* regarding his training schedule leading up to a full practice run of 20 miles during week 23; all this before tapering down 3 weeks prior to the actual race. Amazingly, he completed the race in just over 5 hours. That's impressive in it of itself, considering the fact it was his first marathon. Arguably, had he not laid out a training program involving the use of *phases* (stages), he likely wouldn't be a part of that 1% fraternity. In comparison how does this relate to learning a foreign language?

If you have ever learned a foreign language, you know it comes in phases: Phase - I, Beginner's book; Phase - II, Pre-intermediate; Phase - III, Intermediate; Phase - IV, Upper Intermediate; and finally Phase - V, Advanced. Learning a foreign language isn't easy, though for some, it may be easier than running a marathon.

Likewise, learning is much easier when done in a "systematic" fashion. Learning how to interview is accomplished much the same way, through developing one's knowledge via a progression of *phases*. This process consists of breaking down the interview into 4 - specific phases, each designed to uncover specific qualities about you. For the record, I'd like to reiterate that interviewing isn't an exact science and therefore, you may encounter interviews structured differently.

However - as the author of this book, and one who has interviewed countless times, receiving (exempt) employment contracts with the likes of Astra-Zeneca, Otis Elevator, American Airlines (formerly US Airways), General Electric, Grainger Industrial, not to mention several others; I can unequivocally say with 100% confidence the methodologies expressed in this book are *real examples* and they will work for you.

That said, you can place trust the information presented here will be of "significant" benefit to you at some point during your interviewing career. In fact, you can bank on it! The important thing to keep in mind is that some interviews may not follow the "*exact*" progression of the 4 - phases presented, the knowledge gained herein will provide a substantial base of knowledge one can easily apply to any interview scenario. Let's now provide you an overview beginning with Phase – 1 Introduction.

Phase – I: Introduction:

The introduction phase will be the first opportunity the

interviewer lays eyes on you and vice-versa. Speaking over the phone is completely different than meeting face-to-face. It has its own set of *nuances* explained in mighty detail in the chapter to follow. During this phase, we'll clearly demonstrate how to answer the #1 interview question: *"Tell me about yourself."*

There's more to this question than meets the eye, including preparing a "summary" or "sales-pitch" about you. We'll walk you step-by-step on how to develop an impactful summary that will pay off. Another area of focus employers will pay particular attention to within this first phase will be your previous job history.

During this phase, job history will definitely come under fire as numerous questions will be asked about each, along with the reason as to *"why"* you left. The majority of Chapter 5 will be devoted to providing "fool-proof" responses to these questions, plus making you aware of any possible "follow-up" questions that may arise. Follow-up questions are sure to come, but not to worry as you'll be well-prepared having read the chapter.

Additionally - we'll discuss the little "tricks" interviewers try on you in an attempt to determine your *trustworthiness*. The "subtlety" in your answers will play an important role regarding this; we'll explore it meticulously providing you full clarity on what to say and not to say. Lastly, we'll finish up the chapter with questions you're likely to come across while providing the psychology behind each of them. Next up, an often overlooked part of an interview frequently taken for granted by candidates is Strengths & Weaknesses.

Phase – II: Strengths & Weaknesses:

This phase sounds simple enough, but it's ultimately the #1 area where most candidates veer off path, crash and burn. An in-depth look at the dangers within this area of the maze will be examined along with ways of protecting yourself in keeping you on track for safe passage throughout.

We'll uncover specifics regarding the proper way in responding to the question: "What are your strengths and weaknesses?" Similarly - unlock the delicate balance of giving ample information vs. sharing too much with reasoning behind each. "Weaknesses" will be explored first, identifying the significance of using one versus another.

Furthermore, my Top 10 *"off-limits'"* weaknesses will be revealed along with my "proven" method in constructing your personal weaknesses; paving the way for you to develop your own for future purposes. Afterwards, role-play scenarios will be provided for you to study and reference as needed. Transitioning into breaking down one's strengths will be the focus next. Numerous adjectives will be shared and discussed on whether to include them or not in response to the "strength's" question.

Subsequently, we'll establish rules on developing your "summary-like- statement" incorporating strengths that were "identified" beforehand. Useful examples will be provided at the end of the chapter to be used in a manner of your choosing. One personal note to chew on before moving on to Phase - III.

Before documenting all my interviews, this phase was single-handedly the cause of "my" personal destruction. It wasn't until after creating the interview journal I began to recognize this. You too will spot problematic areas by studying your journal. Amazingly, this one little question tends to trip up so many, yet it happens repeatedly due to it being taken for *granted*. Nonetheless - after completion of

Chapter 5 - you'll be fully prepared in refraining from this.

Next up, Phase - III; where your interview education will take on new heights with the unveiling of the S.T.A.R. technique. After spending time learning all the particulars this technique has to offer, it will ultimately provide you clear navigation through the often feared, *"competency* (behavior) *based"* interview.

Phase – III: Solving a Problem – S.T.A.R. Technique:

The focus of this chapter will be teaching you a proven "methodology" on accurately answering "behavioral questions" related to problems *you* have solved in the past. Many are aware of the acronym called "S.M.A.R.T."; which translates Specific, Measurable, Attainable, Relevant, and Timely; S.T.A.R. is the quintessential acronym used in describing competency based interview questions. The letters represent (Situation – Task – Action – Result).[1]

During a competency based interview, you will be asked to identify a particular *challenge* concerning your personal life or work career, and the steps you took in solving it. I'll provide the reasoning behind its use and share why recruiters considered it the *"gold-standard."* We'll also dabble in the psychology behind using S.T.A.R. in regards to the advantages for hiring managers, particularly in how they assess a candidate's problem-solving ability.

Finding and developing talent, who can *problem-solve,* is crucial to the survival of business as companies have gaps to fill and unsolved problems to fix where new candidates can potentially address these challenges. Employing this technique can very easily *weed-out* weaker candidates not prepared for this type of questioning. However - caution should be exercised due to the reasonable expectation future candidates potentially could be lost simply by the fact they aren't prepared for an interview of this magnitude; included in which - could be their best candidate within the talent pool.

Conversely - this area of the interview process is definitely the "most difficult" to *navigate,* and most candidates will ultimately fail here, due to the difficult nature in the line of questioning. In spite of this, we'll provide you the wherewithal to shine by shedding light on every aspect; including, likely questions asked to explicit responses necessary in keeping your interviewer engaged.

Lastly, the final phase unveiled will be Phase – IV: Why You? Selling Yourself & Overcoming Objections.

Phase – IV: Why You!?!

This phase is all about *"closing"* the interviewer – period! How will you do this? Close your eyes for a minute and ask yourself how would you really sell yourself in 2 minutes? Would you be prepared to answer this question? Are you prepared now to answer this question? For many, this will be the *final* nail in the coffin due to an inability to articulate a meaningful response to *"why you?"* That said, we'll cover the psychology behind this question and provide an exclusive roadmap on how to best tackle it through the sharing of clear and precise examples.

Candidates in a "selling" role will be more adept at handling this bomb-shell question than those who aren't. Nonetheless, we'll address it in depth and offer ways in overcoming fear of selling one's self using my "systematic approach." Included in this will be crafting a "closing-pitch" and providing ways for you to deliver it in a significant way; not to mention exploring the identification and inclusion of personal strengths besides specific accomplishments.

The same, we'll debate whether or not to offer "talking-scripts" beforehand and the usefulness of this approach. Then we'll cover how to overcome objections discovered after asking the "money-question." This section will be very useful and comprehensive to say the least so have a marker handy.

In closing, I'll discuss the importance of having a brag (war) book and items to include inside. Plus, I'll detail my "*worst*" ever interview story; you won't want to miss it. After completion of this final phase, you'll be well groomed in having the knowledge necessary to dominate other candidates vying for the same job. Let's continue our journey by discussing areas where interviews could take place.

Interview Venues:

Now that we've touched on all four phases of the interview process, I need to make you aware of some subtleties in regards to interview location. This will give off major clues as to what type of interview you may incur, which can provide great insight into how a candidate should plan in the long-run. Indeed; taking that into consideration – interviews can be conducted virtually anywhere, but here are the main areas:

Coffee Shop | Restaurant | Hotel | Company

- The premise will remain the same regarding the interview format. However, depending on venue and the interviewer, you may come across variations of the (4) - phases with the possibility of a phase or two being completely left out. Regardless, you'll be prepared either way having learned them all. The good news is, the vast majority of interviews will follow the patterns closely as described.

Coffee Shop:

Coffee drinker? If not, you're not alone. It's possible your interviewer may not be either, hence the reason coffee houses stock other beverages. Having an interview at a café has its positives and negatives. The positives certainly outweigh the negatives, yet there is a danger of falling into a trap of being *too* comfortable, which is the main negative.

It could potentially lend you a false sense of security resulting in the potential for making bad decisions. The sole purpose of interviewing is to uncover who you are through a series of questions and responses and venue will play a large role in determining this. The reasoning behind choosing a coffee shop is *two- fold*.

The first is the fact that the manager may be working out of their home and not have a local office – thus in need of a makeshift workplace. The second could be simply the manager would like to see how you act within a public setting. Other reasons potentially exist as well, but these are the main two. Now let's share the good news.

Having an interview in a coffee shop is more likely to contain the manager who will preside over you; whereas – in an office setting – you may interview with various HR personnel who have no bearing on your career, future wise, other than playing a role during the hiring process. Despite this, the approach should remain the same in all instances with corresponding body language and eye-contact.

Conversely, upon greeting your interviewer maintain eye contact using the *mirror-technique* and follow their lead. If they order tea, you order tea and so on. The interview itself will be less formal and the time frame could last up to an hour as the manager will possibly have 3 – 5 candidates to interview.

The process usually begins with a brief introduction (ice-breaker), then the manager will have you walk through your resume in chronological order stopping you where they deem fit. Expect the manager to ask about your previous jobs and "why" you left, followed in part by potential *follow-up* questions tied to your answers. Finding *tidbits* of information in search of "commonality" will prove difficult in this setting due to the landscape.

Nonetheless – this doesn't give you a free pass!

Some items to look for in this venue: their phone; watch; pen; notebook; glasses (if any); tie; suit; shoes; even the number of sugars they put into their coffee. That may sound crazy, but you're competing for a job, and if there's any way to establish *any* rapport at all, you should definitely try.

You have to make a "connection" one way or another, don't stop until you do. Posture should also be the same with your back straight, utilizing three-fourths of the chair, in order to maintain maximum focus. Upon being asked questions, answer them according to the guidelines presented here and "close" at the end, as per Phase - IV.

Restaurant:

OK - the skinny in regards to having an interview in a restaurant will be similar in nature to the situation above; in that the manager interviewing you will probably be your direct supervisor if you are hired. Consequently - there are many potential hiccups that can occur while dining with a potential employer. Eating at a restaurant can swing the focus away from your resume "content" and shift it towards an unrelated item the interviewer's interested in finding out about you. You can never assume what "that" item might be. I'll explain by sharing a true story about my first ever sales job.

I had applied to a company related to a work associate of my mother. The company was a small regional chemical manufacturer selling various soaps and detergents to clean laundry. They were expanding and in need of additional representation. I had met the regional manager (father of my mother's work associate) at church, who then set me up to meet my hiring manager, named Steve.

Steve decided to have our face to face meeting at a local diner. Little did I know, I had already been penciled in for the job, but had to go through the formality of the interview with one caveat. Upon entering the restaurant the hostess asked, "Will it be *'smoking'* or *'non-smoking'*? Steve looked at me and asked me to make the decision. I answered —"non-smoking."

We then sat down and Steve proceeded to ask me about myself and my previous experience. About an hour after getting to know one another, I was told I had the job, and then to my chagrin Steve informed me, had I asked the hostess for the "smoking" section – I wouldn't have been offered the position. Needless to say; I was quite shocked and a bit disappointed – considering my mother had smoked for 30 plus years. However, having learned the company's insurance policy was contingent on being a *"smoke-free"* work-place, I understood the relevance behind it.

So based on this, it's easy to decipher the one barrier leading to my employment in overcoming was whether or not I smoked. Considering my extensive interview history and employers I've had the pleasure of working for, I've never been scrutinized (to this degree) regarding personal preferences during an interview and hope I never will.

That said, restaurant interviews are a good sign you may

be the *only* candidate being considered, especially if you have a sit down dinner with the interviewer. Pay particular attention, however, in what you order from the menu.

Under no circumstances should you order alcohol unless the manager insists on having a glass of wine or single beer. In this case - limit yourself to only one as the manager could be testing you. More importantly – it's probable you'll have to drive home afterwards so it's in everyone's best interest to have only one. As a reminder, focus on the content of your resume while maintaining good eye-contact and body language. The next venue, offering a lot of versatility for employers, is a hotel.

Hotel:

Hotels offer an array of variations with interviewing in comparison to coffee shops. Not only are they *efficient* in handling large numbers of candidates, but they also have multiple venues within the hotel to choose from. This is one big reason why hiring managers use them.

Another is the fact that the entire interview process from start to finish can be accomplished on the same day. Though the use of additional company personnel may be necessary in doing so, the question on the minds of many could be - why not just conduct them at the office? Good question! The reason can be summed up as such.

Smaller companies might not have adequate space, or they may lack the same level of facilities than a hotel such as: conference ballrooms, break out rooms, full catering departments, or a full business center. Another reason might be because of privacy concerns due to the protective nature companies have of their trade secrets. After all, this is their lifeblood and without it would open the door for risk aversion. Therefore, companies in these circumstances will limit visitation permits for outsiders – thus the reasoning for having interviews elsewhere.

About the process – it could involve a full day of interviewing with multiple company personnel staggered in various time slots throughout the day. It may also include first rounders' or second rounders' previously short-listed from a telephone interview. Whichever the case, it could be as short as one hour to a half-day, or (stated above) take on a full-day.

Usually, the person (recruiter) setting up your interview will give you advanced notice on how much time to allocate, and if they don't, ask! It's a safe bet you won't undergo an all-day process, if in fact you're slated to interview on a week-day. This is due to a large extent to a general understanding among companies that candidates have other work commitments.

The exception to this rule would be in the event of having to attend an assessment center (fully addressed in Chapter 9). Weekends, nevertheless, are often designated for interviews lasting the full day. The reasoning is quite simple. At times, companies need to hire quickly. This can be done through streamlining the process into one day by bringing the entire candidate pool in, having them interview, and then shortlisting a few of them. Afterwards, the remaining candidates will then interview with prospective managers presiding over them. A closer look:

Two interview settings are likely. A large conference room being the *first* - consisting of a quick 15-30 minute interview with any number of company personnel to include: assistants; HR personnel; sales and marketing managers; IT managers; among others. The interviewer is likely to have a *step-by-step questionnaire* (provided in advance) to help guide them in accumulating a "baseline" of information to be used in building a manager's file for conducting second-round interviews. These will likely be held in a more intimate setting such as suite – hence the "second" setting.

The candidates shortlisted will then be exposed to a more intense line of questioning lasting 45-60 minutes. Afterwards, one final round will likely take place soon after (30 minutes) with the remaining candidates being subjected to a small round-robin type interview with existing managers. This final interview will determine a winner by whoever can articulate the best response to: "Why you?" The managers will then compare notes to see who they deem worthy of their next hire. In total, it's likely you'll have 3 interviews.

It's entirely possible to bypass the "conference room" altogether and go directly to the *suite*. If this were to happen, the process could be shortened by one interview. Still – all managers involved will compare notes to see if your answers are consistent with theirs and then the *ultimate* decision will lie upon the manager who will preside over you. The obvious benefit of this interview type is that the company can hire their future employee fast. In comparison - the advantage to the candidate is the fact that they can know their fate (quite possibly) the same day of the interview. Either way it's a win-win for both sides.

In-Company:

The bulk of your interviews will be conducted in this setting as managers have other work responsibilities. Encountering surprises here are infrequent and standard rules of interviewing apply. The *exception* to this would be a case where if the interview type was not conveyed upfront, then the possibility would exist to where one might be participating among others in a "group setting". Nonetheless, I'd ask whoever set up the interview whether it's a group interview or not. A vast majority of the time you'll be informed of this and if not, you'll still have the tools necessary in succeeding, irrespective of this information. In moving on, we'll now begin the exploratory process by digging deeper into each interview phase, beginning with Phase - I.

Chapter 5

Phase – I: Introduction and Resume Review

Many overrate this phase, but don't fall into that trap. All eyes will be on you the moment you step foot in the door. Having to respond to, "Tell me about yourself" – at the beginning of the interview will set the tone early and a weak response to this overused question will send you packing. Don't stress, however, as I'll help you develop a dynamic response to get you shortlisted - which now will be referred to as your "pitch". Other areas of particular interest employers will focus on within this phase will be previous job history and specifics within each.

This will definitely come under scrutiny as many details will be asked of you; including, how you progressed at each job, why you left, and the reason for interviewing now. Your answers must be believable without indulging too much information that could potentially "harm" you.

This will be extremely hard to do *"on the fly"* - so to keep you from faltering during this part of the interview. I've crafted some brilliant responses to assist you in answering these cliché questions. Let's now unveil them along with other hidden secrets one could come across within this first phase.

Earlier, I spoke about my two golden rules - *"building rapport"* and finding *"commonality."* These are in play the very moment you arrive to your interview. Every opportunity to find tidbits of information should be explored as well as conveying proper use of posture and body language. Recall the 7-second rule? To reiterate, you have approximately "7-seconds" to impress your interviewer, so proper voice intonation and complimenting are critical at this juncture. "*Consistency*" in your responses is also paramount and should not be discounted. It is within these first few moments where one wrong move could spell your demise causing the interview to be cut short as a result. Providing "*inconsistent*" answers to like questions asked by various managers is a sure way this could happen. Remarkably - this is the #1 reason why candidates never receive a call- back for an additional interview. It should come as no surprise companies alter interview questions with the intent on deceiving their audience, rewording them in an attempt to determine if one's current responses reflect past replies.

In other words, are you being forthcoming in your answers? In many ways, providing consistency in one's answers yields more importance than the answers themselves. To the chagrin of many, candidates are often blindsided by this and never fully understand the reasoning behind not being asked for additional interviews. This plays large in latter rounds of the interview process.

In fact, I've read on many job messaging boards, like Glassdoor, where young recruits had interviewed with companies I had previously (successfully) and complained about not making it to the last round – wondering what led to their departure. The company in particular (Cintas) relied heavily upon consistent answers from one manager to the other, which probably cost this individual the job. In retrospect, my interview journal was a life-safer for this particular reason. Why such a big deal? I'll explain.

An interview path will usually start by having a phone-screen containing questions like: "Tell me about yourself" and "Why do you want this job?" Additionally, questions about any *employment gaps* will likely be touched upon during this initial screening. Next will be a face-to-face interview with a manager containing a recording (paper or voice) of your phone interview. They can then take this information and dig deeper into areas deemed problematic if they feel it necessary.

This could be catastrophic for candidates unprepared in giving a reasonable response as to why "employment-gaps" exist on their resume, or other issues for that matter. The fact is - some candidates lose track of what they had said previously during the phone-screening, causing the potential for inconsistency in their answers when responding to one interviewer over another. Let's look at a detailed example.

Let's say you interview with Robert face to face, who asks you a series of work-related questions, but is particularly interested in exploring a (possible) employment gap on your resume based on your disclosure of this information during the phone screening. The following week, you interview with Susie, who also touches on the employment gap by using a slightly different version of Robert's original question. This can be accomplished with the 3 different options below:

A) Can you tell me about the employment gap between 2005-2006? (open-ended)

B) So 2005-2006 is blank because you were unemployed, correct? (leading, negative)

C) What type of work were you engaged in between 2005-2006? (leading, positive)[2]

Robert, who was first in asking you about the potential employment gap; had 3 options in which to do so, but in this example let's say he used option B – meaning he did so in a *"leading"* and *"negative"* manner making you feel somewhat embarrassed or a sense of being interrogated. Susie, on the other hand, chose option C representing a *"leading"* and *"positive"* way in which the question was asked.

For instance: "What type of work were you engaged in between 2005-2006," making you feel totally at ease - possibly causing you to say something inconsistent to what you had previously said to Robert. This is *precisely* the reason why keeping an interview journal is crucial! Had you not meticulously documented the first interview with Robert, one can conceive how easily it would be to have veered off course within the maze talking to "sweet" Susie.

Susie's not to blame; she's just doing her job as she's employed to find the best candidate suited for the position at hand. Consequently, both Susie and Robert will compare notes to determine if your answers were consistent based on the information from your resume. The purpose will be to determine if you're telling the truth or not. It's possible that you are, but *inconsistent* answers could undermine this. Why consistency matters can be summed up in two reasons:

First - what company wants a dishonest employee? Second – by expressing erratic responses to various questions during an interview could be a precursor to inconsistent results within your job performance. This would drive multi- national corporations' nuts. It's incumbent upon them to have accurate forecasts for future revenue, thus the critical nature in them having transparency.

After months of partaking in several interviews, in need of my own transparency as to why I was self-imploding, I began meticulously taking notes after each of my interviews, recording them in my journal. Only after a detailed audit did I begin unraveling the mystery as to the cause of my misfortunes. This was discovered by noticing *irregularities* in my responses to many of the same questions being asked by various managers. Upon correcting - my interview results changed dramatically overnight. *Two* important points learned that made a ton of difference:

1st. "Know every square inch of your resume like the back of your hand and be sure your "pitch" is "consistent" each time you're asked about it. Never deviate! Not even once. Have your story down and be prepared to explain any areas deemed problematic, like a gap in employment or a job outside your normal occupation field.

2nd. "Write down every note, detail, sound-bite, reaction, smile, wink, frown, change in body language, or hand shake. No detail is too small. Upon jotting this down, read through it again to see if you're missing anything, add if necessary.

Lastly, anticipate meeting with a "3rd" executive and be prepared to answer identical questions again utilizing the same answers expressed previously. Now let's discuss some questioning techniques you'll likely face in Phase - I.

Ice-breaker questions will likely kick-off the interview to loosen up the mood like: "Did you find the place OK?" Or, "Did you have any trouble accessing the building?" Otherwise - the standard question will be: *"Tell us about yourself."* This is by far the most asked question in an interview.

It's a *"loaded"* question that could break you if you respond in a nonchalant manner, hence the reason for its frequent use. It can *weed out* candidates quickly based on generic, boring responses not relating to the job in question.

Unsurprisingly, interviewing is a professional skill requiring time in perfecting it. Crafting a well-articulated response and delivering it in an impactful way are both equally important. Without it, your chances of advancing through the maze are quite low. This holds true especially when creating a *"summary"* about you - otherwise known as your *"pitch"*- which we'll develop now. Creating your "summary" or "pitch" (1-minute in this case) should not be too complicated. 3 things that need addressing; I call them the 3 "W's":

> 1st: Who Are You? Are you a recent graduate, still in school, or a long-time veteran who's worked

within multiple job sectors? What is it about your education, job training, and experience that make you "relevant" for this job?

2nd: What You Offer? Based on your strengths, skill-sets, and accomplishments – how would this translate into production for (X) company? Include what your friends, manager, or work colleagues would say about you.

3rd: Why Them? Why are you interested in this particular job and company? In other words – what "specific" reasons are you interviewing for this position?

Building the Pitch:

So what's the best approach in building a pitch? This can be accomplished by providing particulars about a fictitious character named "Susie" (below) - a recent MIS grad with honors. Next are the steps used in building the pitch using her information.

– Susie graduated with top honors at U. of (X);

– While studying, learned she has a knack for problem-solving;

— Successfully led 3 projects to completion – which were shortlisted for (X) award;

— Fast learner and loves working in a team-environment;

— Looking for an entry level IT job;

1st: Include an award, skill, or experience that demonstrates relevance towards this specific job; in Susie's case - "top honors"; then add her pertinent experience about projects completed while attending school.

2nd: Add a dynamic skill-set that would mesh well within company (X); follow this up by stating what friends (managers and colleagues) would say about you if asked.

3rd: Share how working for (X) company would benefit the both of you. Let's now build Susie's pitch.

Susie's pitch:

"I recently completed my Masters in Management Information Systems from the U. of North Carolina graduating with top honors. In the process – I discovered an innate ability for problem solving within project management leading to the completion of 3 award winning projects – all receiving national acclaim. My friends would say I'm a quick learner, work well within a team, and always see the glass half full. I'm in search of a company where I can grow professionally and can put my talents to good use and feel that working for (X) would offer me the best chance."

In the text, the 3 "W's" necessary for building a summary pitch have been met for Susie. First – who is she? A recent MIS graduate from U. of North Carolina with "top-honors." Second – what does she offer? A positive-minded team- player able to problem solve with experience in project management. Third – why this company? It's the best fit for her to grow, professionally.

Now let's take a look at another example in Mark: a senior candidate who was recently made redundant and is now seeking a career change. Building a pitch for Mark will be more difficult than in the case with Susie due to the fact of having to explain a "career change."

Recall from our previous example that in order to

satisfy the 3 "W's" in building a pitch, we must demonstrate "who the person is"; "what they can offer"; and "why they are interested in the particular job and company". Mark's information:

- Mark has 10 plus years selling for several Fortune 500 companies;

- Certified in the following sales ideologies: SPIN; Dimension: and Track;

- Top 3 in sales nationally and promoted to regional trainer;

- Displaced in 2010 due to the "Great Recession";

- Wants to transition into a consultancy role.

  1. We need to determine that Mark is relevant for the position by providing an opening statement about his work experience to illustrate who he is.

  2. We must define what Mark can offer. This can be done by listing any professional certifications he has obtained and awards received in order to show a clear career "progression." And then, to drive the point home further, we can add what a

previous manager or work colleague would say about him.

3. Finally, the summary will be complete after adding "why" Mark is interested in the particular company in question; besides the job, and lastly "what" he can do for them.

Mark's pitch:

"I'm Mark and have over 10 years of Fortune 500 sales experience with certifications in SPIN, Dimension, and Track selling. This helped me gain top 3 status in sales nationally and a regional trainer position in the process. After being displaced in 2010, I transitioned from sales into a mentoring role, teaching students soft-skills with a particular focus on interviewing. Students would say I'm passionate, lead by example, and an ultimate problem-solver. If given the chance, I'm confident I can be a champion to younger professionals' to help maximize their potential offering a chance for them to obtain their goals and aspirations through effective coaching, - which is ultimately why I'm here."

There's quite a bit packed into this summary paragraph,

which is to be expected given Mark's tenure. For starters –
we can see Mark used to be in sales with some Fortune 500
companies. Meaning? He's *"marketable!"* Consequently,
since these large companies hired him then maybe
company (X) should "consider" hiring him too. So based
on Mark's summary pitch, we can see that the *first* "W" was
established by Mark having to change careers from sales to
teaching. So who is Mark? A formal salesman turned
teacher – trainer.

The *second* "W" in the summary pitch has been fulfilled
by having listed his *certifications in sales* and how they helped
him thrive within his territory, securing him a promotion.
This shows a natural *"progression"* a recruiter would expect
to see - given Mark's tenure. In spite of this, due to the
financial crisis, Mark was burdened with having to find
employment *"outside"* his normal work domain. Hence –
Mark essentially had to learn a new trade in teaching; aided
by his ability to coach and mentor – previously learned
during his tenure as a regional trainer. So - what can Mark
"offer"? He can sell; train; or teach (Effectively fulfilling
the 2nd need). Now the 3rd and final "W" in Mark's pitch.

So "why is Mark interviewing" and "what can he do for

the prospective company"? Mark is interviewing because he wants to "consult" younger professionals and help them maximize their potential through mentoring and coaching. Specifically, he can provide education that will help pave a way for these young professionals to obtain their life-long goals and aspirations. (Fulfilling the 3rd and final need)

Post Pitch:

After verbalizing your "pitch" - some follow-up questions could ensue before having your work history explored in great detail. For new graduates, the interviewer will likely ask about your classes studied while attending University. For example - Susie's pitch above may yield questions like these:

- o "What were some of your best classes? Why?"

- o "What were some of your worst? Why?"

- o "Tell me some of your proudest accomplishments during school?"

These questions will allow the interviewer to dig a little deeper into your academic career to gauge how you respond in key situations. In Phase – III we'll break down *"solving"* a problem utilizing the S-T-A-R technique and then present more example questions geared to college graduates. Until then, remember the questions above would be a preliminary point to get some essential information about you before drilling deeper with "follow-up" questions before transitioning into Phase – II: Strengths and Weaknesses.

For those with work experience, the interviewer will focus on your employment history and how it relates to the job. This is the reason for knowing your resume inside and out. Any hesitation in the delivery of these details will not reflect positively on you, therefore prepare accordingly. A common question normally asked is: "Tell me about your responsibilities?"

This is already on your resume, but you'll need to articulate it anyhow. Plus, be prepared to answer a follow up question about each position. Here's a sample: "Any change in responsibilities?" The purpose of this question is to see if you have "*progressed*" or regressed.

Regression is a job killer. So pay close attention to this when creating text within the job duties section of your resume, as hiring managers prefer candidates who have taken on more responsibilities within their normal work duties. Another quick and easy, yet tricky, question is: "What did/do you like best about the position? What did/do you like least?"

The reason it can be so tricky is the fact that it's very easy for a candidate to get caught up in being portrayed negatively when answering this question "truthfully." In fact, just by offering up even the slightest details on what you disliked about a previous job could be construed unfavorably, resulting in being painted in a negative light.

This could lead to an early departure keeping you from advancing to the next round. Therefore, one must be careful not to "ramble" upon being asked this question. Look at the following example response. See if you can spot the specific words an interviewer could deem undesirable:

- "I liked the fact I had the flexibility of coming in after 8 o'clock as long as I worked my 8 hour shift."

Pretty easy to see that "coming in after 8 o'clock" could be judged negatively, right? It could be interpreted as being *lazy* and that you frequently stay up late. This despite the fact you indicated having worked your 8 hours. It's always best to say, "You're the first employee in and the last one to leave." So replace the response above with this one instead:

√ "What I liked most was that my managers continuously challenged me by progressively tasking me with increased responsibility, which allowed me at becoming better at prioritizing my daily responsibilities, and thus developed better organizational skills as a result."

Sadly, the interview process is an *interrogation* and designed for candidates to self-implode. Hence the reason why describing unfavorable events in one's career is such a difficult balancing act, as you're required to do so based on past performance. One little mishap could be judged negatively causing you to be passed up for another candidate. Hiring managers are on edge to find the slightest flaw in your *self-assessment* of yourself in order to weed you out. Don't make it easy for them.

The same goes for answering the second part of the question above – *"what you liked the least?"* A yellow-flag should enter your mind the moment you're asked to speak about something you "don't" like. By beginning down a negative path, if one were to venture too far, it will limit opportunities for recovery. So it's best to take the high road. The fact of the matter is, there are positives and negatives to every job, but little can be gained through a lengthy negative rant about a past experience. One standard answer I instruct my clients to use safeguarding them from falling into the negative rant trap:

√   "What I liked least was that I had reached my full potential within the position and had no additional opportunities for advancing my career."

The reality in your mind could be, you disliked your manager, performed at a high level and never received the recognition you deserved, not to mention the pay stunk! We've all been down that road. It's definitely not a good feeling, but a vast majority of people I've spoken to about this very topic has some horror stories (actually funny) they can attest to. It's just the nature of the beast. Finding your dream job is never easy. Having said that – consider the conversation pieces you'll have about all the crappy jobs worked before finding *"the one."* So even though you would like to express those thoughts openly (we all have them) you can't go there. Be professional and take my advice by *using* the sample answer above. Expect any follow-up question to resemble the following:

- "What do you mean by that, could you elaborate?"

- "Can you explain?" Answer back politely in this manner:

√ "Sure – I'd be happy to. What I mean is that the only remaining position higher than my job was an executive level position in which the company did not foresee any expansion for the next 5 years. Therefore – I took it upon myself to look for other opportunities in order for me to continue my professional development."

This demonstrates a few things. One - you're a *loyal* member of the team. Two - you're willing to take on additional responsibility within the company. Three - you're not afraid to seek work elsewhere if the career path suddenly limits itself. Hiring managers love to see this type of initiative. By answering these questions in the manner above, you'll rank high on their list. Let's now prepare you for one question sure to be asked while discussing your work history:

✱ "Why did you leave?" Or, "why are you planning on leaving?" ✱

This question is a bombshell – period! On the other hand, there is a major *opportunity* here to gain a leg-up on your competition. Most interviewers will not *expect* you to say that you're 'happy" in your present position. What would be the point of interviewing if this were the case, right?

However – by answering the question as suggested above via expressing: "you're happy in your present situation" – shifts the *control* out of their hands and into yours. This will undoubtedly raise a few eyebrows with your interviewers, in addition to causing a behavioral change. I'll explain.

Interviewing for a job you don't need will provide *"leverage"* that you don't need them, they need you. Thus – a *control* shift. You wouldn't believe how well this works until you try it. While other candidates will spend their time throwing-up meaningless reasons on why they're interviewing with their impending new employer, you, on the other hand, will have them bending the knee begging

116

for your services after responding with the following statement:

√ "I'm here as a favor to my recruiter as I'm perfectly happy where I am, but out of courtesy decided to hear what you had to offer."

This can sound quite *arrogant*, but much of it depends on the job you're applying for along with how you present it. Even so - it completely throws off the interviewer to where they feel pressure on having to *sell* you on the position. Interviewing is essentially a game of poker where you should never expose your hand to the interviewer. Bottom line - though you may absolutely hate your current job to the nth degree, never allow an interviewer to detect that. By using my example above, the onus will shift towards them in having to express onto you "why them" versus why you.

A Personal Experience Using This Technique:

A classic example of using this was during my tenure with Astra as a sales representative in Orlando, FL. I had been elevated to *"promotable"* status, which meant I was on the *fast-track* to becoming a sales manager. The top brass within the company flew down to Orlando to evaluate me via a series of joint sales calls to get a feel on my suitability for the position.

Shockingly and without warning – splashed over the front cover of Business Week magazine – was a lead-in to the story of our CEO (Lars Bildman); implicated in multiple acts of *sexual harassment*. Everyone knew he was guilty, we just didn't know if the hammer would ever fall. Fell, it did, and hard! The article: "Abuse of Power" details the incredible story of the raucous culture within our company at the time before the fallout. The article can be accessed using the following link with a Bloomberg subscription:

https://www.bloomberg.com/news/articles/1996-05-12/abuse-of-power

Once the news broke, the company *froze* all hires "within" and began replacing managers with personnel outside Astra. I felt it in my best interest to move on due to a large number of sales managers being hired from our direct competitor. Luckily - recruiters knew me based on my sales performance. The reputation of our sales training had also helped in this matter due to its notoriety among medical recruiters, resulting in one scheduling an interview with Ferndale Pharma (Dermatology Company near Detroit, Michigan) at 7:30pm.

I recall the time explicitly, because I was the last candidate they interviewed. Little did I know at that time, upon meeting Julie (District Manager) and Mark (Regional Director), they had already decided on a new-hire from Merck. Consequently - a regularly scheduled 60 - minute interview had suddenly been reduced down to *15*. They had their guy and didn't feel the need to spend more time interviewing additional candidates. For this reason only two questions were asked:

"Why do you want to leave your current company?" My reply: "'I don't!' I'm actually happy working for Astra and have no intention of leaving, but my recruiter persuaded me to come and listen to what you have to offer." Their body-language changed somewhat to a perplexed look, clearly never having heard this response before. Fact was, my response was partially true (recruiter *did* convince me) - but the real story was the company's new HR department was trying to *rid* old blood with new. This inevitably placed me in a precarious situation, but in no way was I going to divulge this.

So I kept my *poker face* on to see this interview through. They then handed me a product brochure allowing me *5 minutes* to look it over as they stepped outside. Upon their return, it was evident (through body-language) they had already made up their minds on another candidate. In fact, I overheard them speaking about their dinner plans later that evening upon returning back to the room, yet they allowed me the courtesy of role-playing a sales call anyhow.

What they didn't know, however, was the fact that I had had 9 weeks of videotaped formal sales training - in SPIN Selling. At the very least, you could say it was brutal! Both Julie and Mark were sitting in the lion's mouth unaware what was about to take place. To this day, it was the easiest (and fastest) interview I've ever been on. The role play went as expected *(I killed it)*, afterwards, Julie then turned to Mark and said, "That was better than in our training." He concurred, then asked the second question: "Do you have a passport?"

Three months later, I found myself flying to Europe (Amsterdam) for my first trip abroad for a week long sales meeting that will resonate with me forever. One year later, I made a $34,000 bonus check and was promoted to East Coast Regional Trainer of the U.S. I completely turned the tables on my interviewers (eventual managers) by suggesting there was little chance in them securing my services. Leading them to cut to the chase, fortuitously giving me the opportunity to prove myself, all in 15 minutes!

Bonus Material:

Afterwards – they both shared that Mark had originally told Julie out in the hall-way to *"blow me out of there, because he was hungry and it was getting late."* – Thus the reasoning for shortening the interview to only 15 minutes. They needn't allow me the chance to role-play, but admitted were *puzzled* by my statement as to why I didn't want to leave my present employer; consequently - wanted to see "what I had."

The reason I got the job was simple, the fact that I was well *"prepared."* Indeed, I was ready for just about any scenario they could possibly have thrown at me. It just so happened to have fallen directly into my "sweet-spot." Fortunately for me that day, I hit a grand slam.

Chapter 6

PHASE – II: STRENGTHS & WEAKNESSES

Think back to when you were 10 years old. Remember the days when life had no worries and carried no responsibilities? Remember playing the *"dare"* game — where your friends would "dare" you to do something really stupid? Did it ever escalate into a *"double-dare"* or a "triple-dare"? Or better yet, the *"coup de grâce – triple-'dog'-dare"* as in the critically-acclaimed film *"A Christmas Story?"*[3]

Remember those days? I definitely have battle scars from dares I foolishly agreed to back then. Dares are a risk and more times than not — bad things happen as a result of accepting them. Answering questions about "strengths" and "weaknesses" is also a huge — "I dare you" (moment).

For many, not much thought goes into this question as it seems so archaic that only an incompetent fool would fall victim to it. Alas — therein lies the rub! These two questions have been around since the beginning of (interviewing) time, due to the very nature they impose. Comically, at times, these questions can trip up the most seasoned veterans when they least expect it. Why?

Because many candidates take this phase for granted and don't prepare for it in advance, which sets the stage for inadvertently saying something out of character, causing an early dismissal from the field. A way to avoid this is by preparing in advance. Preparation is the ultimate "equalizer." It can level the playing field against stronger candidates as long as you know what to expect ahead of time.

Therefore, by tailoring a few scripted responses beforehand will decrease the chances of saying something ill-advised, keeping you in the hunt. Until I began doing this, veering off path was a frequent problem for me, but the interview journal was instrumental in helping me overcome this, through eliminating what "not" to say.

The problems eventually discovered were that I was being "*too*" honest, then it hit me to play the game without *opening* myself up for ridicule. The fact of the matter is - the pressure is on for the interviewer to find the best candidate suitable for the job. The key in successfully moving from one round to the next is by not making "catastrophic" mistakes - offering up information about oneself that could be implicated.

In others words, don't stand out for the wrong reasons, but for the right ones, such as your *charisma*. No one's perfect as everyone has faults, but it's important for the interviewer to discern the fact that identified areas of weakness are being addressed - along with how.

Having a personal *action* plan on the ones you suffer from the most will help demonstrate your awareness of the problem and that you're doing something about it by attacking it *head-on*. Why it's important.

Two reasons: On one hand, it shows you can *identify* specific problems. On the other, it demonstrates you can problem-solve based on *actions* and not words. All companies want problem-solvers – right? Yes, but multinational companies would prefer someone who can actually *identify* a potential problem *before* it "becomes" one. In this way, it could theoretically limit the damage caused by it.

Take for example the financial crisis of 2008. Need we be reminded of that? I digress. Had *"anyone"* (other than a handful of investors) listened to the credence of Michael Burry; hypothetically - the financial ruin could have been far less dire. For those who don't know Michael Burry, he's the one person who *predicted* the collapse of the housing market 2 years before it actually happened; accomplished by noticing irregularities within the sub-prime lending market.

Michael Burry founded hedge fund Scion Capital and was depicted in the film – The Big Short (2015) played by Christian Bale. The movie was nominated for 5 Academy Awards that included best picture, ultimately winning an Oscar for "Best Adapted Screenplay."

Michael was so confident in his analysis, he put (bet) all *his* money into "credit default swaps" (CDS'), a financial derivative used in the backing of home mortgages in the event they default. Only Michael didn't own any mortgages, but the banks sure did.

Another way of putting it, he was betting against the very financial institutions (banks) that were guaranteeing the housing loans – believed to have been sure winners; and betting big (everything he had). To the shock of many around the world, including numerous banking establishments in need of government bailouts, his calculation ultimately came to fruition.

One can now argue based on Michael's story that the ability to *identify* a problem may actually supersede the *solving of problems*. I'll leave that up for you to decide. Regardless, expressing a weakness and sharing how you've taken aggressive action to improve upon it significantly enhances your chances of advancing.

One word of caution though when naming your weakness – shy away from using *personal* weaknesses in respects to personal well-being. For example, it wouldn't be prudent to use a weakness of having conquered a substance abuse problem by attending a drug-treatment facility for 90 days.

This would be filed in the category of *"too much information"* and would likely cause a fatal wound in your chances of getting the job. On the other hand - having an answer like:

√   "One weakness I've been working on is my fear of public speaking – especially in front of large groups. However, in an effort to resolve this I've enrolled in a Toastmasters training program in anticipation of overcoming this. I'm in my third week (currently) and my confidence level continues to soar!"

What can we gather from this answer? The candidate is demonstrating a proactive approach in resolving a weakness by attending weekly training seminars having *identified* a fear of public speaking. One other area I believe is important to note is voice "*tone*." Take notice of the last line in the answer. By ending on a high-note and using the word "soar" – this tricky question has now been answered in a positive and constructive manner.

This shows the interviewer the weakness is being *embraced* and not causing a hindrance. So in response to your interviewer – pay close attention to "tone" as it is every bit as important as the answer itself. Let's now share my foolproof method for constructing weaknesses to be used in your interviews by applying these 3 rules:

I.   Identify

II. Improve

III. Embrace

In creating an infallible weakness - just ask yourself the

following question: Can you "identify" a weakness where you can *"improve"* upon it and *"embrace"* it? It's that simple! If the answer is no, then you have your answer. Start over.

I.   "Identify" it: How? By writing down a list of all your (job related) weaknesses and choosing the one which will least prevent you from doing your job.

II. Can you "improve" upon it? Easy question, for instance: Can you improve upon the "fear of public speaking"? Of course you can! All that's needed is more practice. Practice makes perfect.

III. Can you "embrace" it? If you can't, throw it out and start over. Can you embrace the example above? In other words – do you "acknowledge" that "public speaking" is kicking your butt today, but it won't in the near future? That's the attitude needed when choosing your weaknesses.

Upon choosing them – I recommend formulating fail-safe "scripts" as in the example above before your interview ever takes place. This is part of the "preparation" I speak about throughout the book. The idea of "pre-scripting" an answer to the weakness question may alarm some, but let me ask you: Ever been to a theatrical play; to a movie; a performance; comedy show; or a concert?

Do you think for one second these performers don't *pre-plan*, work off scripts, notes, or music charts? You bet they do, which is why it's imperative to create a pre-scripted answer. Your livelihood is at stake. Now let's look at some of my blunders before necessary changes were made.

As stated before - I frequently self-imploded on this question *unknowingly* until discovering the cause from studying my journal. Have a look at some of the beauties I used to use that sent me packing:

- I tend to procrastinate too much.

- Sometimes I can be "inflexible."

- I prefer doing things my way.

- Sometimes I lose site of the big picture.

Really? It's no surprise I didn't receive a call back! The problem I had was in the fact that I didn't have a clue as to where I was failing. When you're sitting in the hot seat being asked questions in a smooth and debonair manner, it's easy to get caught up thinking you're nailing the interview. After repeatedly receiving a rejection letter, I knew something had to change, I just didn't know what that something was.

After going back through each interview – in search of problematic areas – it always led me back to Phase - II. Why? Because, the constant nature in which I was repeatedly being asked follow-up questions on behalf of this phase; thereby creating a chain-reaction – leading to multiple strings of additional questions, eventually causing my annihilation. I was young, fresh out of University and in way over my head.

Have a look at one of my weaknesses expressed in a role-play, ultimately being implicated, to see how easy a young inexperienced candidate can fall prey to a seasoned interviewer:

I: Interviewer | C: Candidate

I: "Could you share with me a weakness about yourself?"

C: "Uh, hmm, let me think for a second, I'd say I tend to "procrastinate" too much."

I: "Interesting, what do you mean by that, can you tell me more?"

C: "Well, sometimes I wait till the last minute to do things. I wouldn't say I have a habit of doing it, just occasionally."

I: "I understand, can you give me a specific time when this occurred?"

C: "Hard to say, but one time I remember staying up all night to study for a final exam and then fell asleep during the exam!"

I: "Oh my! What was the result?"

C: "I ended up having to retake the class."

I: "These things happen; do you still have a problem with this?"

C: "Not so much, but occasionally when a report is due, I'll sometimes wait till the last minute, due to other priorities."

I: "Like?"

C: "Good question, whichever customer is screaming the loudest (hahaha)."

I: "I see, I'm curious as to how you prioritize your work flow?"

C: "Upon arriving at work, I usually check email and find there's often a "fire" I need to put out."

I: "And your work from the previous day?"

C: "I get to it as quick as I can."

I: "Great! Sounds like you have everything under control."

C: "I do my best, it works for me."

Can you see how the interviewer *led* me to slaughter? My one weakness was *"implicated"* into more problems by simply having a conversation and the interviewer asking follow-up questions. Let's review. My stated weakness, *"procrastination,"* resulted in the following concerns for the interviewer after a series of follow-up questions:

–   Irresponsible (failing class)

–   Lack of prioritizing skills (disorganized)

–   Lack of self-awareness (inability to identify potential problems)

– Lack of a sense-of-urgency (unproductive)

What seemed like a nice conversation, flowing in the right direction, was chock full of problematic statements on my end that raged out of control. Yet, on the other hand, one would think the interviewer was just being nice and kind when in reality the interviewer was *skillfully* dissecting me into pieces. This, because of my naivety and that I offered up way "too much information." Would a *pre-scripted* answer have helped in this situation? Let's have a look:

I: "Could you share with me a weakness about yourself?"

C: "Uh, hmm, let me think for a second, I'd say I procrastinate at times."

I: "Interesting, what do you mean by that, can you tell me more?"

C: "Sure, I sometimes wait till the last minute to do things, but I realize how this has impacted my work and now I'm taking steps to correct this."

I: "I understand, can you give me a specific time when this occurred?"

133

C: "Yes, I waited till the last day to turn in my expense report and the secretary didn't receive it until after the pay period had ended."

I: "Oh my! What was the result?"

C: "I was paid a month late."

I: "These things happen; do you still have a problem with this?"

C: "Not any longer, I learned a valuable lesson after receiving my expense check late – which forced me in having to pay late fees on some bills."

I: "Oh my, has this ever occurred since?"

C: "No sir, I buckled down and created a spreadsheet prioritizing all work related items."

I: "I see, I'm curious as to how you prioritize your work flow?"

C: "I color code everything from red to blue with red being the hottest items and blue being the lowest priority items, then I apply reminders on them when they're due."

I: "And your work from the previous day?"

C: "Completed already."

I: "Great! Sounds like you have everything under control."

C: "I do now – having learned my lesson – which has made me a more productive employee. My managers now have tasked me with additional work responsibilities due to my increased production, which suits me just fine."

Can you see the difference? The obvious difference is that I "*embraced*" the weakness (procrastination) by *owning* it, and by creating a plan of action on how to "*improve*" upon it, my work production increased as a result. For the record,

I would never use "procrastination" as a weakness, because some weaknesses (procrastination) have negative "stigmas" attached to them, so no matter how good your responses to them are, they still look bad on the surface. Now my top 10 list of weaknesses that are insurmountable and 100% "off-limits" during an interview:

1. Lazy

2. Irresponsible

3. Indecisive

4. Tardiness

5. Condescending

6. Emotional

7. Weak

8. Untrustworthy

9. Dishonest

10. Callous

Absolutely positively do not *ever* use any of these, including synonyms. They are virtually impossible to *recover* from so just remove them from your brain. Most are common sense not to use, but it's vital to make that abundantly clear. Remember, you're opening yourself up to major damage when speaking about weaknesses. For some, this is the biggest obstacle to overcome, because you're essentially *badmouthing* yourself.

For that reason - it's imperative to have a detailed plan

on how you're addressing your weakness. The objective is to survive and keep moving along the path to the next interview. Let's help you with that by providing some "pre-scripted" answers in response to some "general" weaknesses below. Included among them are ones that can be applied to "multiple" job sectors, while others have been tailored uniquely to their respective industry:

General – Lack of experience:

"If I were to name a weakness about myself, I'd say I don't have much work experience as you can see by my resume. While some may see that as a weakness, I look upon it as an opportunity for someone to take a chance on me and mold me the right way. Additionally – I set high goals for myself – and believe this trait would yield remarkable results within your organization."

General – too honest:

"Sometimes - I tell it like it is and can be a bit direct. I've been working on this by speaking with a communication's specialist for the past month. He's improved upon my communication skills via role-playing a number of real-life situations. This has led me in becoming a better communicator with my colleagues resulting in delegating responsibilities to them in a more constructive manner paving the way for increased synergy within (X) department."

General - Impatient:

"At times, I can be a bit impatient because I'm a results-oriented guy and set lofty goals for myself. Occasionally - I encounter small setbacks in route to achieving these goals, which can be a bit unnerving. Aware of this, I've taken steps to alleviate it by setting "smaller" SMART goals in order to obtain the larger ones. I'm now more grounded as a result, which has allowed me to establish a clear career path going forward."

IT - Perfectionist:

"Sometimes I tend to check and re-check projects in an effort to ensure accuracy which has led to delays in the past. I've corrected this by changing the frequency of my checks to only one time regarding project precision. In an ongoing effort to safeguard accuracy – I assigned a team-member from each particular project to re-check this aspect before signing off. This has streamlined the quality assurance process resulting in never having missed a deadline since."

IT - Stubborn:

"It's difficult for me to let go of projects that I've personally launched — having spent the time on them and understanding their details. In view of this - I had HR create a special note section in CRM, allowing for project nuances to be recorded within each project, making it easier for me to turn them over to other managers. This has resulted in the ability for me to take on more projects, while keeping a watchful eye on previous projects worked."

Sales - Impatient:

"Sometimes, I can be a bit impatient due to wanting the sale right away, but realize customers aren't always on the same timeline as me when it comes to buying. Consequently - I understand the need to uncover problems within existing suppliers and the importance of demonstrating how to solve them. Even though this process occurs faster for some over others, it has led me to sharpen my pre-call objectives in order to shorten this progression. As a result, sales have increased year after year placing me top 3 in the nation."

By using these scripts above, they will deliver results you're striving for. What to do if you're asked to reference *more* than one? Let's break that down. Interviewers have *tricky* ways in getting you to answer questions, and the weakness question is no different.

In fact – look how presumptuous an interviewer can be in an attempt at uncovering multiple weaknesses through wording the weakness question in a certain way:

o "Tell me "some" of your weaknesses (meaning - more than one)."

Just because you're asked the question doesn't mean you have to offer up more than one weakness. My advice is to pre-arrange at least two and utilize the scripts above. Upon being asked the question, verbalize only one and then if pressed to provide another, you'll have an extra available.

However – under no circumstances offer up 3. I don't care if you're pressed on it, simply state: "I'm sure I have more, but at this time, I can't recall any others." This phrase was all I ever needed in satisfying the interviewer to move on. On a couple of occasions, I was asked to provide another, but never more. Keep that in mind when approaching this delicate area. One last note:

No-one's perfect, so you "must" answer the question. Don't think you can skate by telling the interviewer you don't know of any weaknesses about yourself – because that in it of itself will be your weakness – "no self-awareness." You'll be gone before you know it. Take my advice, learn 3 based on my suggestions above and use them. Other phrases interviewers use in order to pry weaknesses out of you:

- o "What areas would your "previous manager" say you could use a little help with?"

- o "If you could improve one thing about yourself, what would that be?"

Both of these questions are structured in the same manner in getting you to admit your faults. This is why so many *fail* during what most people think is the "easiest" part of an interview. In all actuality – it's one of the most treacherous parts, due to having to speak negatively about one's self. It must be done in a constructive manner, but not in a way that will *reflect* badly on you.

So upon building actionable plans for your weaknesses; structure them in a concise, *consultative* way, demonstrating you're attacking the weakness head-on. This will speak volumes in the interviewer's mind that they would be at a loss for not hiring you. Recapping Weaknesses: Remember to apply my 3 rules when creating your examples:

    I.   Identify

    II.   Improve

    III.   Embrace

In order to identify your weakness, it must be a weakness that can be "improved" upon and one where you can "embrace" it. If not – you haven't *found* the right weakness. Also, pre-arrange a script for the weakness you have chosen. Stick to my "golden-5":

    √   Lack of experience (college graduates)

    √   Too honest (direct)

    √   Impatience

    √   Perfectionist

√　　Stubbornness

These 5 recommendations will *limit* exposure to any "would-be" follow-up questions that could result in the expression of misguided answers causing you not to move forward. Stick with the scripts above so as to offer a safe pathway while traveling through this dangerous (often-overlooked) part of the interview.

Next tip, have knowledge of at least 2 weaknesses with pre-planned scripts and never offer up more than 2 during an interview. If ever asked the "same" question by a different interviewer, keep your answers *consistent* and review your interview journal as necessary.

Lastly – be prepared for the "*trick*" questions in getting you to express weaknesses. They're coming, be ready for them! So upon hearing the question: "Tell me what your previous manager would say you need to work on." Begin verbalizing the scripts above to keep you on track for a successful finish. Now let's turn our attention to "Strengths."

Phase – II: Strengths

Turn back the clock and imagine when you were a kid.

Remember the teacher asking you to bring in something for "show-n-tell?" Ring any bells? I recall being excited on one hand, yet overcome with anxiety on the other, in part due to having to stand up in front of my classmates and present to them. It was all in good fun, but nerve wracking - nonetheless.

It's hard to remember what the actual parameters were, but I recall having to bring in an item of choice and speaking about it for a few minutes. Some kids brought in small pets; gerbils and fish; while others brought in their favorite comic book characters; Superman, Batman, and others. I call to mind bringing in my "Stretch-Armstrong." For those not aware, do yourselves a favor and Google it as it will speak for itself.

The one thing I vividly remember is the feeling of pressure bestowed upon me in having to impress my classmates. Essentially, this was my first real attempt *"selling"* myself. Undeniably, it was clear that my item choice was of utmost importance. Likewise, it had to stand out from the others, yet resonate well with my teacher, due to my crush on her.

I figured by selecting "Stretch," that it would offer the

best chance at delivering upon those needs as well as provide a memorable performance. One that would yield a gold-star from my teacher, and respect from my fellow students. The very nature of interviewing is similar in many ways. Indulge me.

Being asked the question about your strengths is virtually the same as participating in "show-n-tell." You're in effect offering yourself the greatest chance of success by choosing the most appropriate example (strength) that fits you and your skill sets. Let's take that *one* step further by adding "relevance" to the conversation in choosing your strengths. Otherwise, you might not be considered the right fit, though you may be a superstar in your own world.

Another noteworthy factor when selecting your strengths is that you must have a *story* behind each one detailing why they are crucial to the position being applied for. Therefore, upon "pre-planning" your 3-5 strengths, it's key to *research* the company and the job duties required, then build your strengths around them. Points to consider when doing so:

1. Adapt your finest strengths according to the job description in a "summary-like-statement."

145

(Examples below)

2. Phrase your response in the "3rd person – (plural)" as this takes the "onus" off of trying to impress your interviewer, plus your answer will be expressed as coming from your peers. It sounds better, and it leads the interviewer in siding with your associates that yes – maybe you are as great as "they" say you are.

3. Prepare a "specific example" utilizing an identified strength(s) personally used in a real-life situation that was voiced in your summary-statement earlier. This is designed to be a "come-back" response in the event the interviewer asks you a follow-up question like: "Could you provide me an example of when you used (this) your strength(s)?"

    Important Note:

    After giving the "summary statement" – the choice is up for debate on whether or not to articulate your "specific example" to the interviewer. My advice, however, would be to take the lead (without waiting for the follow-up question) and express it in order to match it back to the job description. That way, it will resolve any doubts in your interviewer's mind that you have the necessary skills needed for the particular position in question. An example for a project-management position: "Can you tell me, what are some of your strengths?"

■ Summary Statement:

"If you were to ask my work colleagues – they'd tell you I'm very resourceful and have an incredible knack for sniffing out minor problems before turning into major ones; attention to detail like no other; great ability to bring a diverse group together in accomplishing a common goal; punctual and always deliver on time and on budget." "Great! Could you provide a specific example when you used these strengths?"

√ Personal Statement:

"While a project manager with (X), I was tasked with completing 3 projects with the same deadline. Realizing it to be a potential challenge, I

147

pulled extra members from other project groups and had them assist where needed. Upon discovering a programmer using outdated code, I transferred him to assist on another project where he could best be served, which led to an early completion. This allowed me to use these (free) team members on the remaining 2 projects resulting in early completions as well generating higher profit margins and bonuses for the staff. This won me a promotion to senior product manager where I still am today."

6-strengths were used in the *summary statement* above:

- Resourceful

- Problem Solver

- Attention to Detail

- Leadership

- Punctual

- Dependable

Notice how the "personal example" above articulated most of the *strengths* without ever using the "actual words"? This identifies to the interviewer you're aware of the "job requirements" and have successfully answered their follow-up question. You should always have at least 3-5 personal-examples prepared in your hip-pocket to pull out whenever necessary. Let's share one more example pertaining to a sales representative: "Can you tell me, what some of your strengths are?"

■ Personal Statement:

"If you were to speak with my manager, he would say I'm a producer, self-reliable, and a great goal-setter; and that I have a sense-of- urgency plus a thorough understanding of the sales process; furthermore, an expert in utilizing sales data, tremendous rapport building skills, and determined by never accepting no for an answer."

"Great! Could you provide a specific example on when you used these strengths?"

√ Personal Statement:

"Upon taking over my territory, it was dead last in

the region. I had little time to waste so I created a detailed plan of action to convert as many prospects over to customers as possible. How? By conducting a thorough territory analysis using CRM customer data, which uncovered areas of untapped potential I capitalized on by using my rapport building skills in establishing key relationships. My professional selling skills enabled me to unmask problematic areas within my account base, which I quickly solved, leading to higher confidence levels within the territory. The end result was a triple-fold increase in (year-over-year) sales leading to a national ranking and a President's club nomination."

Did you catch the number of strengths? 7-strengths were used in this particular summary statement:

- Producer

- Self-Sufficient

- Goal-oriented

- Sense of Urgency

- Trainable

- Likeable

- Motivated

The "personal example" above is another scripted answer one can use for interviewing. We can clearly see the candidate has a *"sense-of-urgency"* and doesn't require any hand-holding. Managers love hiring candidates who don't require an eternity to train, which would eat up valuable selling time. I definitely recommend communicating in the text of your response the fact that you don't need to be "hand-held." On the contrary, you're a "fast-learner" and can take the ball and run with it.

Other key strengths in this response include that this candidate is *"likeable"* and understands the importance of building "key relationships." With any successful sales position, this is central in *repairing* territories that are in the tank. As a hiring manager, this would be the first quality I would look for in rebuilding a territory. One reason the territory could be in the crapper is because (former) clients are buying from people whom they do "like."

Furthermore – the response also demonstrates that this

candidate is well- trained, in both sales and on how to put company resources to work for them; for instance - the CRM tool the firm has spent a fortune on in order to maximize sales opportunities. The old cliché of the "80/20-rule"; where 80% of your business comes from just 20% of your clients - is a steadfast rule in business - important to adhere to for any successful (territory) renaissance to be gained. Having a solid grasp in the targeting of prospects based on CRM data will help satisfy the 80/20 rule, necessary for allowing the transformation process to begin.

Recapping Strengths:

1. Create a "summary-like-statement" based on your individual strengths tailored to the job.

2. Phrase your summary in the 3rd person – (plural). It will have a more meaningful impact on your interviewer by stating what "others" believe to be your "strengths."

3. Prepare a "specific example" in anticipation of having to respond to an interviewer's follow-up question or questions.

In our next chapter, we'll take your interview skills to new heights by offering you an inside look into how recruiters and hiring managers assess candidates; by breaking down the "competency-based-interview", while unveiling ways on how to conquer it - utilizing principles established in the construction of Phase - III.

Chapter 7

PHASE – III: SOLVING A PROBLEM – S.T.A.R. TECHNIQUE

Take a look around you. No matter the venue; whether you're amongst friends, business associates, or even strangers cheering your local sport's team on; the general topic of conversation is seemingly on inventing a new way for one to gain a competitive edge. From Wall Street; to the sport's world; to the corporate world - the search for perfection (via data) lives on.

For Wall Street companies, it's discovering a new trading algorithm to increase investor returns; for sports' team owners, it's finding a unique scouting method - centered on statistical analysis in search of finding the perfect athlete; for the corporate world, it's securing the best interview method to find world- class candidates.

The common denominator amid the above is the relentless pursuit of inventing a "fool-proof" method to find elite talent. Let's face it, better players, and in this case candidates, make for better results. Statistically over time this will play out. Exceptions do exist, but the latter holds true. The big question remains whether or not it's possible to "game" the system?

To say it another way, does the opportunity exist where a person or company can improve the odds of success by uncovering a better tool or method, based on the study of data? Many Wall Street firms believe so; in their attempt to do just that by throwing large sums of money towards the recruitment of data scientists and engineers; holding PhD's in Math, Computer Science, and Physics. All in an ongoing effort to game the system, for better decision making, to obtain higher returns for their clients.

In the sport's world – the Oakland Athletics (A's) in '02 attempted to game the system through their use of a personalized version of "Sabermetrics"; created by their general manager, Billy Beane, in an effort to assemble a *competitive* ball-club after being saddled with the 3rd lowest payroll in professional (MLB) baseball. What is Sabermetrics you ask?

"Sabermetrics is the search for *objective* knowledge about baseball through analysis of statistical records."[4] In layman's terms – it's the study of "objective" data vs. "subjective." In other words – player personnel decisions are exclusively based on "raw data" (or statistics) versus "gut-feelings." Not to belabor the point further, but indulge me one last analogy to paint a clearer picture.

Let's say you were a baseball scout and witnessed a player you deemed the next Babe Ruth, while their raw data showed otherwise. Under the guidelines of Sabermetrics, the player wouldn't be considered. This method helped the Oakland A's win a division pennant and league best 20 straight games in the process. They made it to post-season, but fell short in the end, losing out to the Minnesota Twins in the American League Championship. All of which was depicted beautifully in the #1 National bestselling book by Michael Lewis named "Moneyball – The Art of Winning an Unfair Game."[5]

The book cast light on how *Sabermetrics* could level the playing field for low market teams compared to the likes of the New York Yankees (triple the payroll of the A's). The success of the book (story) later developed into a Hollywood film – starring Brad Pitt (2011).

The movie was a box-office success (both financially

and among peers) having received 6 Academy Award Nominations, including Best picture and Actor. In the process, Billy Beane was accredited for single-handedly transforming baseball via his "customization" of Sabermetrics - which has now come to pass as "Billy Ball."

He essentially took the nation's past time, turned it on its head, and has forever changed it.[6] In comparison to the corporate world, could these efforts somehow be duplicated?

> Shockingly, during the editing of this book, the A's record of 20 straight wins was "eclipsed" by the 2017 Cleveland Indians after winning 22 straight, nearly 15 years (exact) to the day of Oakland's famous run. Despite this, however, Cleveland's fortunes ended abruptly after losing out to the New York Yankees in a 5-game series during the first round of the American League Playoffs (ALDS).

The "Moneyball" of the corporate world is categorically - the *"competency (behavioral) based interview"* a.k.a. "Structured Interview." This is accomplished through use of the S.T.A.R. technique in finding suitable candidates based on a number of job related (measured) "competencies."

S.T.A.R. is an acronym for "Situation – Task – Action – Result." It's the *quintessential* method for describing a problem solved in your past, both personally and professionally. A quick glimpse at the type of questions you'll encounter with this technique:

- "Tell me about a work related situation on when you encountered a problem and the steps you took in solving it."

Think about that for a second. How would you answer that? Would your answer contain a clear and concise *"plan of action"*? Or, would it be a jumbled mess of entangled "Uh's & Um's"? Welcome to the world of Competency-Based- Interviewing using S.T.A.R.! As for your answer to the question above, save it and we'll revisit it after breaking down the meaning of each letter.

S-Situation:

What was the situation? Specifically, what was the setting (people, place, mood, atmosphere, time, and purpose) like and the events that took place during. Furthermore - what is "your" reasoning behind voicing this and what lessons can be learned from doing so?

They are a million ways to *dress* this up, but the bottom line is you need to "set-the-stage" for what's *about* to be described and the reason for describing it. After identifying a *solved* problem – the focus must shift from recounting the "situation" to articulating what *"tasks"* were necessary in rectifying it.

T-Task:

To put it in basic terms, what "Tasks" were needed in fixing the problem? In other words, what was the mission, job, assignment, undertaking, chore you completed? What did you have to do to make this "problematic" situation better? What was the ultimate goal behind smoothing things over?

A-Action:

What did you actually "do" (*physically* and *mentally*) step by step? Employers want a (verbal) "flow-chart" of your plan on how you *"took"* action after a situation didn't go as planned. In essence, they want to see how you think, tick, and problem solve. We've all heard the phrase, "Actions speak louder than words" – right? Using the S.T.A.R.

technique is a bit of an oxymoron.

On one hand, you will have had to have performed some meaningful tasks; in contrast, it will be necessary to "articulate" the actionable steps you took in completing those tasks in a precise and systematic way - all on demand.

That, in and of itself, will not be an easy task if you have never *"performed"* these actions previously. Having said that, it's easy to see where a candidate could be *exposed* in having their (job-related) weaknesses uncovered while being asked this *style* of questioning.

This is why this interview format can be lethal to an unsuspecting candidate. For this reason, I'll unmask this methodology by presenting explicit workable examples you can use in preparation for designing your own. Additionally, I'll explain the psychology behind its use in great detail, permitting better insight in helping you prepare for this increasingly difficult form of questioning. Now the final letter – "R."

R-Result:

What was the "final" result, the final outcome, conclusion or ultimate solution to the problem you solved?

Put simply – how did the story end? What came of it? What eventually was gained by the company, you, your audience from the "specific" action steps taken previously? Was the outcome positive? Were there any major break-throughs? These are the questions one must ask themselves while pre-planning.

The beauty in using this technique is you can also apply it to your daily life in conjunction with formulating SMART goals. Perhaps, it's now easier for you to see why employers use this technique, but we'll explore why in the following paragraphs. Afterwards, you will have a thorough grasp to the power it offers to both candidate and the interviewer. The reason for its use will now be explained as we direct our attention back to our original question above:[7]

- "Tell me about a work related situation on when you encountered a problem and the steps you took in solving it."

Based on the information above, would you "now" change your answer?

Hopefully your answer would be a resounding yes! But, let's explore further. With this type of interview – there's no "*winging*" it – hence the reason why recruiters and hiring managers use it so frequently. Another reason for its use is that up until the S.T.A.R. methodology evolved, it was hard to determine how a candidate would *fit-in* with an organization based on just a resume (CV).

For example, many high paying positions such as medical doctors and attorneys believe their Academic Qualifications (on CV) speak for themselves without having to go through a series of unnecessary interviews. However – a huge benefit to using S.T.A.R. is that it *forces* candidates to demonstrate their *competencies* "in person" through the sharing of real life work experiences – a CV or resume cannot do. This ultimately provides transparency on whether this person would be a good fit or not - regardless of profession.

The upside for the employer is that they can systematically ask very *pointed* (open-ended) questions related to the job. Thus – creating an effective way of exposing a candidate's "*limitations*" in performing the job in question, based on the candidate's "own" work experience, or "lack" thereof.

The downside for the candidate is that a competency

(behavioral) based interview can *negate* rapport building efforts already established in Phase - I and Phase - II. If you have great chemistry with the interviewer and then appear dumbfounded after being asked a "behavioral question" in handling a problem with your previous employer, then suffice to say, the interviewer may be apprehensive moving you forward.

On the other hand, if the job requires the need to *build* "rapport" - as with many sales positions and customer oriented jobs – then you may get a pass. Nonetheless, if you were to continue *stumbling* in answering them, the interviewer would have no other choice, but to send you on your way.

This is precisely why it's necessary to be aware of it and to have a plan of attack upon encountering this interview technique. It's the *crème de la crème* and the Moneyball equivalent to *"objectively"* critiquing interview performances for the purposes of shortlisting candidates. If you aren't fully prepared, your chances of advancing are slim.

Furthermore – it's very difficult to *game* the system – especially if you *lack* the precise skills the interviewer is in search of. In light of this, a list of questions *strategically* designed in determining whether you're suitable or not will have already been prepared prior to your interview. So one must create well-articulate examples (based on work experience) beforehand; relating them to the job- opening advertised in order to properly prepare oneself in countering them.

Hidden psychology behind its use:

In Chapter 5 (Phase – I: Introduction | Resume Review) we spoke about the need to have *consistent* answers to deem a candidate trustworthy. To reiterate, during the interview process it's likely the candidate will come across multiple interviewers asking the same questions, but in various ways.

If for any reason the questions are not being answered consistently, then it's *plausible* the candidate may not be telling the truth (in the interviewer's mind). In all honesty – they *could* be telling the truth – though their answers may be *suggesting* otherwise. This will be up for the interviewer to debate. Notwithstanding, it's better to err on the side of caution by ensuring uniformity through whatever means possible.

Likewise - If a candidate *cannot* provide consistency in

their answers, can they be counted on to deliver predictable work results? Therein lies the question. What's more, can they be trusted in a role *financially*? These questions begin to creep up if the former is said and true. One can circumvent this by preparing a few pre-scripted "case-studies" from past employment detailing specific involvement expressed in the S.T.A.R. format.

In this manner, upon being asked a *behavioral* question related to a previous work role, one could seize the opportunity by confidently communicating a well- crafted answer pertaining to the desired job skills. This could, perhaps, satisfy the interviewer in your ability to perform job (X), enhancing the chances of being short-listed. One can now see why the use of S.T.A.R. is so prevalent among employers. Because of this, a candidate's *integrity* will come under fire unless responses are being successfully expressed in this format.

Lastly – if you're speaking in Uh's and Um's after being asked a pointed question failing to produce any "specifics" in your response, it may appear you are indeed full-of-it, thus deemed an unemployable candidate. Therefore, avoid using them at all cost. One final note regarding S.T.A.R.:

❋ It isn't mandatory to express (or say) each letter (S-Situation; T-Task; A-Action; R-Result) literally, because the interviewer will believe the candidate is unaware of this method anyhow. So it's in your best interest to play dumb by not referencing them. Nevertheless - the flow of the responses (story) must be "similar" to the language representing the letters. Otherwise, the interviewer may not believe them.

Summary: S.T.A.R. serves major benefits for both the "interviewer" (Company) and the "candidate." Company benefits can be summed up asking two questions:

1st: Did the candidate's responses include previous job "situations," and did they demonstrate adequately enough the skills necessary to perform job (X) without disclosing any weaknesses?

2nd: Did the responses flow naturally in a systematic way following the S.T.A.R. methodology, less any Uh's and Um's?

If yes, then it's reasonable in assuming the candidate is both *trustworthy* and has the required skills necessary in fulfilling the job, positioning them as a suitable candidate; thus benefiting both company and candidate - to the tune of having confidence in moving them forward.

Candidate Benefits:

S.T.A.R. technique can impact the candidate both professionally and personally. The S.T.A.R. methodology offers a logical approach in expressing a problem solved in either one's professional career, personal life, or both. It provides a practical and meaningful way on how to structure responses to difficult questions detailing one's personal contributions in a clear and effective way.

Furthermore – it coincides well with SMART and the ability to set goals helpful in achieving personal and professional milestones. It can be used by virtually everyone, and should be an intricate part of a candidate's pre-planning strategy in preparing for the interview journey that lies ahead of them.

Behind the Scenes Look:

Since the reasons why multi-national companies use this technique have now been revealed, let's unveil what happens behind the scenes on how candidate's interview performances are "recorded" and documented in order for companies to make a hiring decision.

First off – many multi-national companies will have an *"interview guide"* created on their behalf by a company specializing in employment services. This guide could come in three different versions, each representative of an interview. Therefore, it's conceivable a candidate could partake in 3 competency-based interviews, on 3 separate occasions, conducted by 3 different managers, using 3 different interview guides.

The guide is likely to be structured in a way providing the interviewer step by step instructions on how to conduct the interview from beginning to end. For starters – it's probable a "Preparation Checklist" will be provided to assist personnel on precise action steps to take before interviewing the candidate such as: reviewing resumes (CVs) for employment gaps and noting any questionable facts that seem unclear; next - preparing a list of behavioral questions (from a pre-determined list) matched to the candidate's work experience.

Afterwards, a step-by-step outline is likely to be provided on how to open (start) the interview. This could include: how to greet the candidate; explaining the purpose of the interview; describing the agenda, job functions and asking whether the candidate can do them or not; it's possible the interviewer will be required to state some basic company facts before expressing the fact that questions will be directed at the candidate and their answers recorded by the interviewer. Afterwards – the interviewer will transition from the opening of the interview to gaining background information.

This will likely involve asking the candidate about their educational background followed by questions about (any) work history. We covered specific work and education related questions that could arise in Chapter 5 (**Phase – I:** Introduction and resume review). A review of this will reveal questions like, "What was your favorite and least favorite subject, and why?" And, "Talk about your job responsibilities and the reason you left company (X)."

Candidate "responses" will be recorded in whatever means necessary for company personnel to have free access to, in ascertaining your viability for advancing. As the interviewer is documenting your replies, the candidate should simultaneously be making *mental* notes as well, in order to record them into their interview journal afterwards.

Several "behavioral questions" are likely to come next in determining one's ability to meet competency requirements as the interviewer takes notes in the S.T.A.R. format. In all likelihood, "Vital Abilities" for each *competency* will be available for the interviewer to "checkmark" in order to evaluate your performance. Let's take a look at some examples:

Let's say the "Competency" necessary in satisfying (at least) one job requirement is "Resolve & Vigor." The Vital Abilities listed for the interviewer to check off during your example (response) to the behavioral question could look according to this:

Vital Abilities Checklist:

√   Persistent

√   Stays on track

√   Doesn't give up

√   Maintains an audience

√   Deflects negativity

Then the behavioral question could be something like this:

"Tell me a time when you had created a goal and abandoned it due to something out of your control."

The interviewer will keenly listen to your response and check off the appropriate *vital abilities* above, while documenting your answer in the S.T.A.R. format on their interview-guide. However, it's imperative in understanding that some of the behavioral questions being asked of you are *misleading* in that they purposely try to throw you off course by leading you in the wrong direction.

The question above is no exception. In providing an answer to this particular question, a surprising number of candidates would actually "list" a time when this had happened to them. Under no circumstances do you ever admit to "failure" – *ever!* You must always show the interviewer a never-die-attitude; otherwise, you're outta there. So below would be a more appropriate response to the "behavioral" question above:

√   "For me personally, I've never abandoned a single goal. In fact, I "embrace" a challenge. While

171

working at HP, our team was given a special promotion to sell 100 printers to our partners within 30 days. I created an action plan that included my top clients who had previously purchased printers in our region. I presented the promotion to them and followed up daily each week. By the deadline, our team was short 10 units, but I never gave in expecting HP would extend the deadline, which they did; allowing me to sell the additional 10 units. Our team won first place and received 2 paid vacation days."

Based on this answer – you can easily "check-off" each of the vital abilities above indicating this candidate has "Resolve & Vigor." One can also see the "structure" in the candidate's answer via S.T.A.R. and how might the interviewer document this on their interview guide sheet. I'll show you how an interviewer would do that now:

SITUATION / TASK:

While working at HP, candidate had a promotion to sell 100 printers to HP partners, deadline of 30 days.

ACTION:

Created an action plan listing top users; followed up daily every week. By deadline – team was short 10, but candidate was "persistent."

RESULT:

Candidate assisted team in selling all 100 units and won 2 free vacation days.

CANDIDATE NOTES:

Candidate deflected a negative situation by demonstrating a positive attitude in which he/she didn't give up, maintaining focus on the task, remaining persistent and ultimately persevering.

For some companies – at the bottom of their interview guide sheet – there's a section where the interviewer can give a final mark (depending on the rating system by the company) of 1-3 or 1-5 on their ability to meet the required competency. This will be based on two things:

1st: Did the candidate meet the "Vital Abilities" in their response to the behavioral question?

2nd: Did the answer follow the S.T.A.R. technique to the point their story is believed to have happened?

If *both* apply, then the candidate should receive a "high mark." The competency-based-interview is likely to continue in this format to determine if you meet a number of "competencies" involving a plethora of behavioral questions. Let's share another potential example.

Example 2:

Let's say the next "Competency" being measured is: "Dedication to Self- Improvement." The vital abilities may be the following:

√ Self-aware of individual needs for personal growth

√ Demonstrates a willingness to learn

√ Accepts constructive criticism

√ Uses criticism to better one's self

√ Applies learned skill Behavioral question:

- "The only constant in life is change. Tell me a time where you had a work related change and how you adapted to it?"

Response:

√ "Two years ago my manager (Phil) retired and the

company brought in a younger manager (Leon) from a direct competitor - who was an expert on Salesforce.com (our firm's CRM system). After a field ride- with, Leon suggested ways of better targeting my customers in improving my territory performance (though I was 2nd in the region). He suggested watching the in-company webinars to polish up my targeting skills. So I promised to do so within 2 weeks and get back to him afterwards. Within the first 2 webinars – I discovered a high potential client and began calling on them – which led to a large order propelling me to first in the region and 5th nationally. I now train other reps on how to use CRM, which has led the company to fast- track me into their managerial program."

Did the candidate meet the 5 -"Vital Abilities" in the above response based on the behavioral question? I'd say *clearly* yes. Did the response follow the S.T.A.R. technique to where their story is believed to have happened? Again, I'd say clearly yes.

Taking this into account, if I were the interviewer, I would *mark* this candidate with a "5" given their clear ability in demonstrating a "Dedication to Self-Development." Upon adding this latest realized competency, this would now satisfy two *competencies* with an "unknown" number left to complete. Therein lies the problem.

Only the company and your interviewer will know for certain. It's possible to have 5 or more competencies asked of you. It too is conceivable that one of your responses may not suffice; leading the interviewer to asking *another* behavioral question within that same "competency" to gain clarity in your ability to perform it.

General rule is that an interviewer will explore your ability to perform 2-3 competencies *per* interview. This could also include being asked questions about the same competency already covered in previous interviews, which is why "consistency" matters. To add, it would be advantageous to have *two example* answers for each competency prepared in the event you are asked to provide another example related to the competency in question.

Closing the Interview:

Instructions on how to close the interview, for all

intents and purposes, will be provided to the interviewer that may include a "Final Checklist" resembling something like this:

→ Ask the candidate for materials (brag book) in making their case for being hired.

→ Review any notes in determining if more information is necessary during the next interview.

→ Ask any last minute follow-up questions to materials presented by the candidate.

Next will be your opportunity to ask questions. We'll speak about when to ask the *money-question* in the next chapter. That said – it would be wise to have a couple of questions at your disposal to ask. Two of my favorites are:

1) "Can you tell me which qualities your top employees possess?"

2) "What challenges could I face if I were to land this job?"

Asking these last 2 questions will set the stage for you to counter with a dynamic response by matching your skill-sets with those the interviewer shares as pertinent traits within their present employees. Also the fact that you have the wherewithal to solve any issues they state as problematic for them currently. We'll explore this at length during the next chapter.

Post Interview:

The candidate's information from the interview guide will then be compiled onto an A-4 size *"information grid"* listing all "competencies" available for assessing. Only the competencies explored during the actual interviews will be rated. "Every" interviewer must categorize each response in the S.T.A.R. format into their appropriate competencies, then rate them according to the candidate's ability to perform them. All documented at the bottom of each competency page. The marks will then be transferred to the information grid to determine a "Consensus" on whether or not (X) competency can be performed.

One additional factor potentially involved in the final appraisal is: "Observed behavior" of the candidate during the competency assessment. Observed behavior could also be a part of the evaluation process measured through two particulars: "professionalism" and "communication." Both may be listed on the data sheet to aid in determining a final consensus consisting of the following "vital abilities":

Professional:

√   Dresses appropriately

√   Displays professional demeanor

√   Speaks confidently

Communication:

√   Organizes the communication

√   Maintains audience attention

√   Ensures understanding

√   Applies learned skill[8]

Once all the "Consensus" information for each competency has been tallied – a "Yes" or "No" decision will be made and documented at the bottom of the data form. If you don't receive a call-back within a few days after your interview, don't panic, because it's likely the company is still compiling the results. However – if two weeks elapse and still no contact – then it's safe to say the company has moved forward without you.

❧   I've had companies contact me one month later

after interviewing, but this is rare. The logical reason being the fact they short listed other candidates only to discover (after the next round of interviews) they were less suitable – thus the reason for "adding" me back into the candidate pool.

Summary:

We pulled the curtain back on the "gold-standard" of face-to-face interviews by having introduced "competency-based-interviews" and the underlying effect "behavioral questions" have on them. Conversely, we unveiled the S.T.A.R. technique and established why multinational companies use it so frequently; plus shared the benefits for both the candidate and hiring manager. In the process, the hidden psychology behind using S.T.A.R. was exposed in determining candidate trustworthiness via ability in providing consistent answers.

In closing, we provided an exclusive "behind-the-scenes" look into how multinationals record interview information in assessing whether a candidate is a "Yes" or "No" vote through the use of an employee "interview-guide." Now we move onto the final phase of the interview process, Phase – IV: Selling Yourself.

Chapter 8

PHASE – IV: WHY YOU?

Phase - IV is about driving the *stake* into the hearts of the other candidates and *closing* the deal by selling yourself and overcoming objections. Accomplished through delivering an Oscar like award-winning speech that not only answers the question – "Why You?" – but will resonate within the hearts and minds of your interviewers causing a lasting impression long after its conclusion.

This (sales) pitch should be a mix of your top strengths (1-3) and personal achievements directly related to the job. The most important aspect of your pitch is that it must convey how these chosen attributes would benefit the company, and upon your hire, you would deliver on that.

Only one opportunity will present itself and if any loose ends linger, this will be your last chance at sewing them up. This final phase affords you the chance to complement all your greatest attributes, expressed previously about yourself, to cement the fact that you are the right candidate for the job.

With that in mind, it will also be your biggest individual moment on stage in trying to accomplish that goal; with the real possibility of throwing everything down the drain, in the event you deliver a dud of a performance. Moreover - I cannot stress how paramount it is for candidates to prepare a well-articulated "speech" in advance. To draw a comparison to help illustrate, let's take a look at some famous lines vocalized in some of Hollywood's finest Oscar Award winning films:

Forrest Gump:	"Life was like a box of chocolates, you never know what you're gonna get." - Tom Hanks[9]
Dark Knight:	"Why So Serious"! - Heath Ledger[10]
Jaws:	"You're gonna need a bigger boat." - Roy Scheider[11]

The Godfather:	"I'm going to make him an offer he can't refuse." - Marlon Brando[12]
Terminator:	"I'll be back." - Arnold Schwarzenegger[13]
Shawshank Redemption:	"Get busy living or get busy dying." – Tim Robbins[14]

Oscar Award Winning films are won based on many culminating factors besides a single line in a film. However, if you were to ask moviegoers about these particular films, my guess would be the first word from their mouths would begin with the corresponding quotes above. Why?

Because, the actors in these films delivered these lines with such precision, and in such a resounding way, they produced an everlasting impact that will live on for generations to come. This is indeed the precise goal in Phase - IV. To deliver an Oscar-like performance leaving an *unforgettable* impression on your interviewer.

Psychology Behind it:

By asking the question "Why You?" your interviewer is

essentially saying *"show me something."* Show me what you've got compared to the others. It's a real life Hunger Games[15] situation, and you're up! Another less dramatic reason is that it puts you through yet another "test" to gain valuable insight in making an informed decision about you compared to the others.

In contrast - sometimes the interviewer's just looking for a little something extra as they want to be "wowed." Can you blame them? After all, it's their reputation that's on the line as most candidates shortlisted will be well qualified. Therefore, the final decision will come down to the one candidate with the better *closing argument* on how their skills and personality match up best. So time spent on perfecting this "closing" pitch will loom large.

Pitch Crafting:

This involves a *3-step process* based on the position you are applying for. Initially, it will be necessary to identify what the specific requirements are. Afterwards, you will need to customize your pitch accordingly based on the 3 rules below.

First:

Determine that inner gift (trait, skill, success, accolade, accomplishment or experience) that differentiates you from everyone else. For me – it's uncovering a problem and providing a workable solution. For others, maybe it's something similar. That will be up for you to decide, but it must fit you! Don't try to be Superman when you are Spiderman. In other words, don't say you're great at something when you're not! Interviewers will see right through you. Dig down deep and find what it is about you that makes you who you are.

Second:

Use the key *attribute* you have determined above and let it serve as your "Core" - then build on it by adding strengths and personal successes pertaining to the job. You can change your strengths according to the job, as maybe strengths for Job A will not coincide with Job B. However – you will want to keep your "Core" feature intact while *interchanging* other pieces (strengths and personal experiences). For me - "uncovering problems and solving them" is my niche. So in building my pitches – I always use this as my *anchor* and build upon it.

You should have a few pitches in your arsenal (with different "Cores") allowing you flexibility for different job types. Think of your Core as a Lego board. You can easily take one block (strength) and affix it to a separate Lego "board" (Core). I tend to stick with my Core attribute as it practically interchanges with just about everything. Shoot for a similar attribute or just use mine. Remember, however, to prepare oneself in "backing-it-up" through personal examples using S.T.A.R.

Third:

Use the "KISS" technique. KISS is an acronym for "Keep-It-Simple-Stupid." To say it another way - keep it *short* and *concise*. No more than "90 seconds." That's quite a long time if you speak without the other party interjecting. Time yourself.

Pitch Scripts:

Should or shouldn't you have a pre-planned script? We touched on this in Chapter 6 – Strengths & Weaknesses regarding "performing-artists". Personally, I believe it's critical to have a script ahead of time. The gray area is in whether to *memorize* and recite it word-for-word the interviewer's behalf. This is up for debate, but I regress by turning back to the Hollywood films' examples above.

The actors in them had scripts and most definitely memorized them. Perhaps they improvised or maybe not. Nonetheless — they had a foundation to work from — and so will you. You can choose to either *adlib* portions of your script or just play it safe by delivering it word for word.

As your comfort level increases through practice, you can venture out and improvise as you see fit. That's the *choice* you have, but it's crucial in having a working copy of a few tailor-made "closing-pitches", which include a Core, a few strengths (1-2; no more than 3) and any other accolades you deem worthy in distinguishing you from the others.

Preparation before the interview:

Coach (Bruce) Kreutzer (Miami Heat assistant coach) inscribed these words on the back of our uniform hoodies: "Prepare Today for a Better Tomorrow." Coach "K" — my former high-school basketball coach — instilled upon us the key to winning was determined by the level of preparation put-in beforehand. The relevance to the latter is in the fact that one must prepare a game-plan (scripts) ahead of time and be fully in-tune with it lockstep.

After which, upon receiving the call (audition) to sell oneself, the time you put forth in preparing will enable you to deliver an Oscar worthy performance. After generating your scripts – create a few variations and role-play in front of the mirror, paying close attention to your voice reflection and body language. Recite and role-play your scripts till you can do so in your sleep. Then, and only then, will your body-language be in perfect *tune* with the delivery of your message.

Delivering the message:

The delivery of the message is every bit as important as in the message itself. Therefore, after being summons to speak, take a deep breath and hold your chest up high. Have both feet firmly on the floor - shoulder width apart – locking eyes *through* your interviewer's with the intent of seeing through the back of their head. Then calmly access the respective (job) script from your brain's filing cabinet and begin delivery while exhaling simultaneously. Final notes on delivering your message:

The candidate's body-language has to *convey* the same message as the content within their script. It also needs to exude confidence in order to sell the interviewer in what you're offering. In my honest opinion – one cannot do this unless they recite the bulk of their script prepared in advance. Oscar winners, in many instances, are remembered by *one* single line in their films that made history. This isn't Hollywood, but the two are very similar in many ways.

Actors have to audition for their roles, as do candidates. Likewise – actors spend a bulk of their time studying scripts, role-playing in front of mirrors, hour by hour, day by day perfecting their roles, so why shouldn't you? Interviewing is a professional business, and only the professionals will remain after the dust settles.

Overcoming nerves:

Preparing in advance will eliminate most of your anxiety – as "knowledge is power!" By the time you're asked this question you will have spent hours, days, if not months preparing for this moment: reading this book, fine-tuning your CV, writing exceptional cover letters; participating in phone interviews and face-to- face interviews; writing solutions to problems using S.T.A.R., and creating an Oscar-like "closing statement" as to why you! There will be no room left for any nervousness having properly prepared for this question well in advance of it appearing.

In spite of this – it's important to continuously remind yourself that you *deserve* this considering the above. For now it's your time and no-one will take that from you. Mentally, think about beating your chest while taking a deep breath inward. Then access your pitch and let it fly. I'm confident if you follow this format – it will be you standing in the end. Trust in yourself and seize the moment – for it's yours!

Final Thoughts:

After answering the question: "Why You?" Your heart will be racing and you may be thinking, "Finally", it's over! Not quite, but almost! Listen carefully to what I say next – as this will be the stage where your interviewer will allow you to ask questions. This is the precise time where I believe you must follow up your Oscar-like sales-pitch with a "trial-close" question to determine if there are any *objections* to you being hired.

Some industry experts disagree with this approach; asking the Money Question as a *first-line* question – but I'm in the camp that as long as it's "worded" in the right manner (examples in Chapter 2) there is no reason not to ask it "at this time."

The interviewer will have just heard your plea on why you, now it's time to shore up any reasons, *why not you.* Therefore, ask the question without hesitation, because you never know if you'll be afforded time for another. Listen carefully for any objections, follow the rules in Overcoming Objectives below.

Overcoming Objectives:

In Chapter 2 - we briefly touched on this and the significance of asking the *"money-question."* It's important to know where you "stand" in determining the likelihood of getting the job. In order to do that you must "ask"! Otherwise, you may lose out on that one opportunity to overcome the real reason standing in your way of getting hired. Overcoming objections is not the hard part – *discovering* them is!

It's conceivable an interviewer will express their objections *directly*, especially if you've done a good job in building rapport (beforehand). On the other hand, if you haven't and the interview is coming to a close, this could be your one shot in resurrecting yourself – potentially pushing out another candidate. So it's crucial in asking where you *stand* along with having pre- scripted answers prepared to counter the 3 most popular objections below:

- Lack of Experience

- Job Gap

- Lack of Education

This is fairly easy to overcome unless it's for a technical position. In that event, it would be wise to lay out a detailed plan of action on how you propose to obtain that particular skill lacking, assuming the time frame to do so would be reasonable. For all other positions, "on-the-job" training will be provided, so merely expressing a willingness to learn can easily *overcome* this objection.

Taking that into account, it's vital to "sell" this to the interviewer, or they will choose a candidate who does. The over-all goal here is to articulate reasons why passing on

193

you would be their biggest mistake; using your charm and related skill-sets. The second most popular objection that is much harder to overcome is a job gap on a resume.

Job Gap:

The glory days of working 30 years for one company and retiring within that same company are long gone. Globalization, the explosion of social media, plus pressure within the tech community to create the "next big thing" is placing mounting pressure on recruiting firms and companies to find skilled personnel. What does this mean to you?

If you're in the IT field, not much in terms of having to overcome an employment gap or even a job nevertheless, as you'll likely be in high demand. Whereas, let's say you are in sales and was recently made *redundant* outside of your control. What would be the best way on how to explain this?

I believe in the adage "honesty is the best policy" – so I would explain the reason for the gap. Then provide transparency on what you did in the interim to acquire work. During the financial crisis of 2010, a large majority of my friends lost their jobs. For many, it took months for them to find employment, exacerbated by the fact of having an employment gap from not finding work soon thereafter.

Fortunately, though, many recruiters overlooked these blemishes on their resumes with the understanding of how damaging the crisis actually was, thereby making the process slightly easier. Nevertheless – many (worldwide) were still severely impacted including me, who ultimately had to switch careers out of necessity.

The important thing here to bear in mind is that interviewers will want to know what you did during this time off. Did you take a sabbatical and travel the world, or were you relegated to finding work immediately for financial reasons? In either case, it would be beneficial for you to share something constructive you did in improving your hire-ability. This could include:

- Enrolling in a language course; accounting course; sales-training course; or even a coding course;

- Taking a real estate course and becoming certified;

- Working part-time;

- Getting a new accreditation as an automotive mechanic;

- Learning a new trade.

A unique opportunity presents itself here in that you can disclose how you were able to work on some personal *weaknesses* (in between jobs) mentioned in Phase - II. This will go a long way in demonstrating self-awareness and that you are "productive" with your time, both on and off the field.

Having said that – it should be obvious (by now) you need to pre-plan this in advance. For this type of objection, there are no second chances in getting it right. If you stumble out of the gate with the reasoning as to why you had a gap in employment, you are finished. Let's provide a sample scenario with an appropriate response:

Scenario:

Candidate had worked in sales for 5 years and has been laid-off for 12 months; has spent time searching job boards daily, handing out resumes in-person to prospective employers, calling friends for referrals, visiting the unemployment office, and enrolled in an intensive Spanish course for 16 weeks. Your "pre- scripted" response could look something like this (utilizing S.T.A.R.):

I: Interviewer | C: Candidate

C: "Do you see any concerns or pitfalls from our conversation today that would hold me back from moving on to the next round?"

I: "I'm just a bit concerned about your gap in employment, other than that, no."

C: "Thank you for pointing this out. In 2012, our company restructured and laid-off 30% of its work-force. Territories were eliminated (mine included) through consolidation. Our company's success relied heavily on the Latino population and Spanish language. Therefore, I felt it necessary to take a 16-week Spanish course in order to help me become a more effective communicator. While searching for work and exploring friendly referrals, I dedicated myself at night to studying Spanish. This led to a noticeable improvement in me being a more patient person. After finishing the course and receiving a B2 level certification, more job opportunities in the form of face-to-face interviews have come my way."

With this pre-scripted answer, all the bases have been covered. It explains the *reason* for the gap, what you did in the interim, and how you added a skill-set while looking for employment. Notice at the end where I added how it's helped me secure more interviews? This would be a big eye-opener for the interviewer. Because, it shows they are not the only game in town, and that you have other options available in the event they decide to pass on you. Let's turn our attention now to education.

Lack of Education:

Education is the cornerstone in the development of one's career path. Overcoming a lack thereof will prove to be difficult, yet on the other hand, the possibility does exist. In lieu of not having the required education, the only true way of circumventing this is by establishing what you do have will out-produce another candidate who does have the required education.

Experience can outdo just about any objection, but you have to word it in a way that will "bridge the gap" caused by your lack of education. For example, if you don't have a Master's degree in Business, but understand Accounting and Finance, articulating this in a convincing manner would increase the odds of successfully sidestepping this. Ultimately, many employers will forgo the need for a Master's if you can demonstrate your experience will adequately allow you to perform the job.

Therefore - never allow this to come in between you and obtaining a job. Most company managers would take experience over education any day of the week. So if it comes up, be cool and use your pre-scripted responses. That said, if the job is technical in nature or science based, this would be an area where this requirement wouldn't be waived; as many government offices require you to possess this in order for companies to maintain a permit to conduct business.

Let's provide an example where you could *outmaneuver* a candidate with a Master's. Let's say you have 10 years of nursing experience and you're up against a candidate with a Master's in nursing. Your response to the objection could be:

I: Interviewer | C: Candidate

C: "Do you see any concerns or pitfalls from our conversation today that would hold me back from moving on to the next round?"

I: "I'm just a bit concerned about your lack of education. The job requirement is for a Master's in nursing and I'm not sure if we can get around that."

C: "I understand your concern; however - please allow me to justify my reasoning for being here. As you can see, I have over 10 years of nursing experience, which includes a variety of rotations in various hospital departments comprised of working with some of the most renowned physicians world-wide. In fact – I was instrumental in helping Dr. X with a personal case study on X that was published in JAMA. Not only am I perverse in many procedures throughout the hospital, but I'm also an expert on medical "coding" - ensuring that your physicians will get paid. What's more is that this has taken me years to learn, something a person with less experience will not have. Therefore, by hiring me, I could immediately pay dividends without you having to spend hours training me. Do you have any other objections before advancing me to the next step?"

Pre-planned scripts similar to the one above need to be prepared in advance for these *three* popular objections. This will provide you a solid platform to work off of in the event you need (want) to improvise. Here are examples you can customize to your own liking:

Objection – Lack of Experience:

"Thank you for the input and please allow me to respond. Though the other candidates may have more experience than me; rest assured - they don't have the drive and passion that I do; in fact, upon taking over my territory, it was the worst performer nationally. Within 12-months I was able to turn that around due to problem solving and working day and night (including weekends) to give my customers the service they deserve. This led me in receiving employee of the month for 6 consecutive months. If given the chance - I could do the same for your company as well."

Objection – Lack of Education:

"Thank you for your candidacy. Education is a passion of mine, and while I wanted to stay in University to complete my Master's, a job opportunity arose (after completing my Bachelor's) I couldn't pass up. It allowed me to obtain expert status within this field by working on select case-studies not possible had I remained in school. Considering this - I could put this first-rate experience to work for your company if given the chance."

Objection – Gap in Resume:

"I'm glad you brought this to my attention as this unfortunate incident enabled me to acquire a foreign language in the interim while looking for work. After being laid-off, I began searching for work immediately by means of personally handing out resumes and working friends for referrals; meanwhile - learning Spanish nightly for 16-weeks. After completing the course with a B2 certification, it helped me in becoming a more effective manager. This in turn increased my communication skills within the Latino community, aiding me in successfully gaining work shortly thereafter."

To Sum Up:

Asking the money question will yield 3 common objections requiring a matching response. These responses should be tailored using clear-cut information from your resume that will turn the adverse situation discovered into a positive one.

In the event you were unemployed and learned a new skill in the interim, share how that improved your hire-ability. Follow that up by asking if any more concerns exist that would keep you from moving on to the next round. Handle any additional concerns that may surface accordingly. Let's now share the importance of maintaining a "war-book" - otherwise known as a "brag-book."

War (Brag) Book:

Some call it a "brag" book and others a "war" book. Nonetheless, it's meant to describe a folder, envelope, book, or what have you to keep all your work related accomplishments in one place. A bounded copy is provided to each employer I interview with for the purposes of them having easy access to all my accolades.

Not only does this re-emphasize me having

organizational skills, but also provides the convenience of my interviewers not having to fumble through a bunch of individual papers, risking them becoming angry in the process.

What to include:

A war book should include anything you deem pertinent that will give an employer a better idea on why you would be a good match. For those of you in sales, if you have any sales "data" you could get your hands on, this would be helpful in backing up your claims made during the interview. Present the information chronologically, demonstrating how you progressed from start to finish. Examples could be in the form of:

- Job performance appraisals;

- Certificates of achievement to include: Sales training, Accounting, Google, Programming, or IT;

- Market share data against competition;

- Sales data versus your peers;

- Any awards (no matter the size) including: employee of the month, an award for making the most calls, teacher of the month or year, salesperson of the month or year.

You get the general idea - no award is ever too small. Include them all, so you can then use your personal war-book as a brochure to demonstrate what's pertinent to your audience. So if you're in accounting, maybe you have had to take a few training seminars in SAP. Copies of this should be in your war book and then upon request, you can easily validate the fact that you have SAP experience by presenting them your certification.

Another example:

Let's say you work in IT as a project manager and have received multiple awards and are in search of a position that would suit you better. These (awards) should be included in your war book. If it's a trophy, photograph it and include that as well.

One last example:

Suppose you work in sales. Demonstrating a paper-trail of a positive *progression* on how you were able to increase sales since inception would be a nice touch.

Upon creating your war-book, it's important to

recognize everything in it and have a *story* behind it. I recommend putting all items in chronological order (as discussed above) reflective of your resume (CV) for ease of use in walking the interviewer through established work history.

This enables you the opportunity to point out accolades within each job, painting a clearer picture of the steps taken how you improved upon yourself. Multinational corporations are all about progression not "re"gression.

When to use it:

One should carry their war-book with them at all times due to the unpredictability of face-to-face interviews. I've been on interviews, where the interview was cut short for unexpected reasons, and the interviewer abruptly gave me one minute to make an impression on them.

In these instances - I always reverted to a specific place in my war-book pertaining to the job and person interviewing me. So always make sure you carry it with you, and determine "beforehand" who your *audience* will be; for instance - IT, Accounting, Teacher, or Sales among others. Then have one to two specific achievements you are most proud of and why.

Furthermore, make certain you can walk the interviewer through your book in a clear and concise (story-like) manner. This piece of evidence is solely designed to prove you're worthy of the position. Therefore, use it as such and after the conclusion of the interview, hand them a copy as you would your resume at the start. This will go far when other candidates fail to do so. Managers appreciate viewing something other than just a resume.

Intellectual Properties:

If you include anything that could be construed as an infringement on intellectual property, I'd definitely use caution in adding it. It's up to you on whether to include it or not, but if you do, I'd refrain from leaving a copy behind. In fact – the same (pharm) rep I spoke of earlier, which used to wear a bottle of fragrance into the allergy offices, would also try and discredit my product by showing bogus studies to physicians without ever leaving them behind.

Thankfully, the vast majority of the physicians shared this with me and never paid it any attention. That said, just err on the side of caution, because you can always blackout information deemed questionable while still maintaining the gist of your award. After all, it's your performance we're referencing here; you've worked hard for it, so include it as long as it's not a blatant cause for concern. Now - what you've all been waiting for, my worse ever interview story costing me a $100,000 per year dream job.

My Worst (Ever) Interview Story:

For many people, securing a $100,000 a year job would be a dream come true and I'm no exception. As I boarded the plane from Orlando to San Francisco, the only thought crossing my mind was simply to follow the tips I've disclosed in this book. They had helped me succeed in gaining all my previous job offers, so why abandon them now.

The company (Schering-Plough) was by far the best opportunity to have ever presented itself for me at that time and I was keen on closing the deal. My interview journal accompanied me during the 5-hour East to West Coast flight. This offered me time to review notes from prior interviews conducted by local managers.

Upon learning I'd be speaking with 5 executive managers individually, I anticipated I may have to repeat answers from the original interviews, which included two phone screenings and two face-to-face meetings. The phone screenings were standard; questions about previous employment and how I obtained my largest sale - covered easily using the S.T.A.R. technique.

Conversely - the two face to face meetings were much the same. After expecting a more difficult process, in hindsight, I consider these particular interviews to be some of the easiest having ever encountered. Nonetheless, I was prepared either way. An important piece to add was the fact that their local managers were already *aware* of me, from competing against them in their other (RX – prescription) division.

Schering had originally cornered the RX market regarding nasal-steroid inhalers, as they were first to sell into it. They reaped the success of this for years, and because of this, physicians were ready to try something new. This helped expedite the process in me taking a large chunk of market share away from them in short order. Another reason for this was in the way they sold to physicians.

Schering-Plough (now Merck) trained their reps on how to *"detail"* physicians using studies and product brochures than actual (consultative) selling. "Detailing"- in the sense they'd take a pen, point to a particular area of interest and speak about it; whereas — we used a consultative approach via (SPIN Selling) asking open ended questions in search of uncovering problematic areas for the purposes of providing physicians our solution.

In this particular case; Rhinocort - it worked well. However, to their defense, physicians had been prescribing their nasal inhaler (Vancenase) for years, so switching them over to Rhinocort was a synch. The success of which was neatly tucked away in my war-book. Including myself, there were a total of 3 candidates vying for this position.

Normally, I'd want to know who the other candidates were, but on this occasion it didn't interest me in the slightest; given the confidence I had from the previous interviews and successfully selling against them in the past. Apart from this, I did manage to run into the other 2 candidates; a girl and a guy, but never saw them again. It didn't matter as I was locked in and prepared for just about anything they could throw at me.

Truth be told, the feelings I had about participating in the upcoming interviews were merely for show, as I believed they had already penciled me in for the position based on prior success against them. Only time would tell if this were proven to be true.

Despite this, I felt it would play no bearing as long as I followed my game- plan, which consisted of all the ideals shared with you thus far. Upon arriving in San Fran, we were put up in a Marriott, all expenses paid, allowing for one more night of studying my notes before setting off at 8 am.

The agenda for the day was to interview with 5 different managers one-on- one including: [Marketing Director, VP of Sales – Hospital Division, National Accounts Manager (Managed Care), Director of HR, and National Sales Manager]. But as luck would have it, the National Sales Manager canceled due to a scheduling conflict, which now meant having only to interview with 4 managers.

This was then further reduced down to 3, as both the Marketing Director and VP of Sales joined in to conduct a 3-person group interview. Astonishingly, this left only the

National Accounts Manager and Director of HR remaining for a one-on-one interview. Each of them lasted for about 45 minutes; and my earlier thoughts on being penciled in for the job was appearing more evident. This based on body language and questions they were asking me.

Most of which were about me and my interests and how I was able to obtain such fast results within my territory. For which I replied - the importance of having a call objective for each visit and the need to document all details during the call upon exiting the building. I also expressed the significance of creating a next-call-objective (NCO) after each sales call.

Then the National Accounts Manager (first interviewer) – asked how I would handle obtaining formulary approval for a drug not approved? Though I didn't have any personal knowledge, I had prepared an answer for this particular question by speaking with a former rep experienced in this area.

I felt a bit exposed, knowing he could have exploited me on this, but after being asked if I had any questions for him, those thoughts soon dissipated as fast as they had appeared, lifting any weight previously on my shoulders.

Afterwards, he asked if I had any questions concerning the job which I responded, "What are some potential concerns you see within this territory and industry as a whole?"

The industry was oncology and the product [Intron-A (interferon-alfa-2b- recombinant)], used to treat non-Hodgkin's lymphoma, which had just been approved by the FDA. So it was reasonable in assuming this manager was under the gun to produce results fast based on knowledge within the industry.

This wasn't newsworthy as many of my original trainees during my tenor with Astra had been clipped the first 6 months due to non-performance. In spite of this - his position would traditionally be offered a bit more of a grace period.

Nevertheless, his response mimicked how crucial it was in getting off to a fast start. He stated the importance of getting a running start out of the gate and I concurred by nodding my head in acknowledgement while feeling exuberant in anticipation of getting the job. The interview concluded shortly thereafter.

In looking back as to why he didn't press me on my lack

of working in national accounts, could only be explained by the stellar recommendation I had received from the National Accounts Manager at Astra, documented in a referral letter. Having seen this letter in my war book convinced him I was his guy, which was later confirmed by his response to the money-question having no real objections, stating: "I'll have to compare notes with my other colleagues, but at this point everything looks great." I didn't press further as his body language clearly matched the positive tone in voice, satisfying my need in not asking any further follow-up questions.

Next up was the VP of Sales. Upon walking into his office, Julie (Marketing Director) approached us and asked if she could join in to "get it out of the way." Admittedly - I was perplexed hearing this as I had kept expecting the worst and it appeared to be getting easier. I recall the VP of Sales (Ken) having a framed autographed jersey of Dwight Clark of the San Francisco 49ers on his wall. The man who single handedly ripped the hearts out of every Dallas Cowboy fan after making (arguably) the most famous "catch" in NFL history – now simply dubbed – "The Catch."

Much to the surprise of many, I attended the same high school as Dwight, who also had a younger brother 3 years ahead of me. Needless to say, I felt as though I had just struck gold! I then began sharing personal stories about the competitiveness of Dwight towards his younger brother (Jeff) – acquired through various channels within the high-school ranks. All I could think of next was - Jackpot!

We talked mainly about sports the entire interview and Julie could barely get a word in. Of all places in the world to be in at that given moment; offering up the grandest tidbit of information one could possibly have dreamed of was divine intervention. Everything was going according to plan – then rolled in Dick.

Dick was head of HR and on a tight schedule. He worked in the office next to Ken's and cordially said, "Whenever you guys finish up, notify me and I'll ready myself for the interview." Julie asked one last question on my reasoning for wanting to work at Schering. After answering, they thanked me for my time and said they looked forward to seeing me again. Their body language also confirmed with what they had said; giving me the feeling that I was that much closer to pay dirt and the feeling was justified, albeit a bit premature.

I asked for their cards on my way out and gave them a firm hand-shake. They then walked me over to Dick's office next door. I was on an emotional high, believing without a shadow of a doubt, both Julie and Ken were a Yes vote. Despite this - I still had one more path to travel before exiting victoriously. Admittedly, it was immensely difficult regaining focus after discussing Dwight. The greatest athlete ever known to have come through my high-school (3500 miles away) with strangers I had never met before; strangers, nonetheless - who had my fate in their hands.

The gravity of the situation quickly presented itself upon meeting Dick; a man in his late 40's to early 50's; a bit overweight, sporting an untidy beard and glasses. He wasn't at all what you'd expect for a man in that position, considering the industry.

Notwithstanding, he had this distinctive uniqueness in the way in which he expressed himself. Tantalizing in a manner to where his tone was lax, yet razor sharp in frankness undeniably captivating to the ear. It was frustratingly difficult to read him from the start, unlike the

216

others before him.

As he eased himself comfortably in his chair, placing his legs on the corner of the table he asked, "So Kevin – how do you feel about your interviews thus far?" My response was not as quick as one would have hoped for, because of time spent pondering the question. The real question in need of answering, however, was whether I should be forthright and say (thus far) it's been the easiest job interview I've ever been on. Or, should I lie and say it's been the most difficult?

I sided somewhere in between by selling the idea that this job was the perfect fit by stating: "Interviewing today has further solidified my belief in knowing this position is the perfect fit for me." He followed by saying: "We feel the same about you; otherwise, you wouldn't be here."

Again, I was back on my high horse and taking a victory lap. Dick had a copy of my war book and resume in front of him, but was particularly interested in my market share figures against his own company as I had 40% of the nasal (steroid) inhaler market, including a large majority of that coming from Schering.

He asked how long it took me in acquiring it and to describe the number of steps in doing so. During my reply, he bowed his head down in order to see over the top of his glasses. [Recall in Chapter 3 (body language) I mentioned a potential problem if the interviewer had their hands on their glasses.] Fortunately, that wasn't the case here as his eyes were intensely locked with mine, similar to two gunslingers squaring off waiting for the first to make their move.

It was an eerie feeling I hadn't experienced the entire day. I didn't know what would come of it, though one thing for certain was my return back to Orlando was scheduled to take off that afternoon. After factoring this in, I expected the interview would last no more than 30-45 minutes. Not a second later, Dick reiterated precisely the same by saying, "I know you have a plane to catch and we'll have you on your way shortly — as 'this is just a formality.'"

Upon hearing those words, I was already popping the champagne in my mind; aware of the fact this job would soon be paying me more in salary than I had had in all my previous positions. My inner self was in celebratory mode, while my outer remained a bit subdued. I began thinking how great that upcoming plane ride was going to be, including the number of mini-bottles I could down before arriving back in Orlando.

However, in the back of my mind, I kept seeing that look in Dick's eye. Needless to say, it was concerning. The nature of how penetrating it was, yet how nonchalant his body posture was by having his feet resting up on his desk. It was conflicting to a large degree, yet I paid it no attention, as I was already counting the number of dollar bills that would soon be raining from the sky upon signing the contract.

It was at that exact moment when Dick asked the most basic of interview questions one could ever have asked. A question so elementary even an imbecile could manage without any misfortune. That, my friends, is why they ask the question! It was at that precise moment where I obliterated the most important rule written in this book for you to follow. That is — "to never let your guard down." After all, this was *just a formality* and I had a plane to catch, right? Wrong! The question: "Describe a typical day for you."

There you have it. Easy, right? Not so fast my friends!

219

So I began by describing my day from the time I woke up (6:00) till the time I went to bed; adding I do a 30-minute workout every other day, followed by breakfast, then out the door no later than 7:30 to ensure I'm at my first appointment by 8am. Then I said, "I always game-plan the night before by targeting at 'least' 15-20 physicians daily with the goal of making 8-10 quality calls."

I was still trying to get a read on Dick during the process while he nodded his head in approval. I took this as a positive sign, though it was his first. I felt now, if I just remain on cue and avoid any missteps – the job would be mine. Dick was beginning to show his hand and my inner self turned up the music in response. Then he asked: "And for lunch?" My reply: "In an effort to build rapport with my top prescribers, I schedule as many one-on-one luncheons as I can."

Again, he nodded while keeping his feet on his desk. The celebratory music had begun to ring louder in my head, and the plane ride back was shaping up to be one epic experience. I continued by describing my afternoon work routine (more or less the same as in the morning).

In the process, I began thinking how I would close out

the conversation. I discerned I needed a big finish, and my mind was clambering to find one. Just one problem - I didn't have a working "routine" in the afternoon, except for making a few physician calls, and a pharmacy call or two; Truth be told my afternoons varied broadly more so than my social life.

Meanwhile - the pressure to ensure consistency with my answers was evident, as my mind began to race frantically on whether I had offered up any information about my routines in the past. On the surface, turbulence had begun to appear, though you wouldn't have recognized that via Dick's body language, looking as stiff as a wax museum celebrity.

For the life of me, I couldn't believe I hadn't prepared myself for this question ahead of time. After reviewing tons of notes and pre-scripted answers to various behavioral questions, one would think I would have covered such a basic essential. Noooppe! By the looks of it, Dick's question asked was a no- brainer, but as with all interviews, there can be many unpredictable moments.

Having said that, while expressing my afternoon activities I felt the need to detail how I had acquired that

40% market share (stamped in my war-book) by often working well past 5 o'clock. Not only would this help paint me as a workaholic, but would also provide the close my brain was yearning for in order to close the deal.

The point of no return:

So Dick continued to sit as stiff as a log, feet still affixed to the table, while I shared how I would take in Haagen-Dazs to the front desk staff (mid-afternoon) to build rapport with hard-to-see physicians. Dick perked up and slightly began nodding his head, before curling his lip to indicate a job well done. While doing so, I then blurted out - unsuspectingly of any repercussions - "I knock off at around '4:30 pm' to enter additional call notes into my notebook, before finishing up around 7:30-8 pm."

Up until that point, the turbulence had been choppy, but nothing to write home about. In fact – I vividly recall thinking how well he'd perceive the fact I was working till 8pm. Yet, after making this one slipup - articulating "four-thirty" - 8 pm and my job chances had vanished. I was now in the midst of a hail storm with little place to hide; for it didn't matter whether I had said 8pm or midnight. In Dick's mind – he was stuck on - F-O-U-R | T-H-I-R-T-Y!?!

It didn't hit me at first, but soon after, I felt a weird vibe, followed by an unforgettable reaction that still haunts me to this day. Dick's feet descended downward with his eyes enlarging in the process. While positioning his feet on the ground, he then pinned his hands to the desk for leverage, extending his torso upwards and said with a distinctively loud voice: "You 'knock-off' at 4:30!?!"

My inner self screamed for help, but there would be none. Dick's hands now "firmly" on his glasses, mouth half open, and a look as though someone had urinated on his desk. My mind scrambled to think of a way to rectify the situation before all was lost – but all had been lost with one Freudian slip of the tongue. This was a lost-cause with no chance of making it out alive. How could an honest expression of time events have caused such a reaction just steps away from the finish line?

Answer? *"F-O-U-R | T-H-I-R-T-Y!?!"* In the HR world these words are taboo and considered career suicide. Knocking-off work prior to 5 o'clock "in the field" will always be construed by HR as a lack of work ethic, regardless of nature. By the same token, HR within multinational companies will mainly concern themselves with an employee between the hours of 8 to 5 -irrespective of job type.[16]

This is considered company time and saying anything outside this realm would be cause for immediate dismissal. The endless amounts of hours you may have put forth (on weekends, at night, and on vacation) may matter in the minds of your friends and family, but will fall on deaf ears within the HR community. Therefore, be aware of this fact, otherwise, you could fall victim.

How it ended:

Dick looked at me with clear frustration in his eyes, as the only remaining obstacle between me getting the position was simply a rubber stamp that ultimately had to come from him. Despite this fact, I came up short by encountering an unforced error at the most inopportune time. Dick stood up and thanked me for coming, extending his hand as the air in the room began to dissipate.

The fact was — the air in the room had long dissolved before this moment. I felt a sense of having been purged already from his mind, and him thinking of the next item on his agenda for that day; for it was still fairly young - all things being considered.

With that in mind, a brief glimpse of hope had entered into my consciousness that perhaps I could be misreading the situation as I hadn't received an official "no" - directly. Much to my chagrin, however, I wasn't offered a chance to ask questions, which was concerning, yet I still kept hope alive.

On the return flight I retraced every step, breaking down question after question while analyzing the corresponding answers. Still, "F-O-U-R | T-H-I-R-T-Y!?!" kept echoing throughout my brain, wreaking havoc on the little hope I had remaining. In the meantime – partaking in the consumption of 5 mini-bottles during the return helped comfort the situation, and provided insight for me not to succumb until after I had spoken with the recruiter, which occurred the following morning.

Upon hearing the first sentence out of his mouth left no doubt on where I stood. The question he asked wasn't, "How did it go?" Or, "Well, what do you think?" It was simply: "What in the 'hell' happened!?!" My gut - uncertain from the mini-bottles or the recruiter's question - hurt so badly I nearly threw up. My $100,000 (a year) opportunity had vanished as quickly as it had appeared. That little glimmer of hope I once had was forever crushed.

Nevertheless, I remained positive and focused on how I could use this learning experience to my advantage. In the end, it taught me the importance of never taking the essentials for granted, plus it reinforced my number one rule to - "Never Let Your Guard Down!"

Chapter 9

THE DREADED - ASSESSMENT CENTER

Assessment center? "What is an assessment center" gets repeatedly asked by candidates throughout smaller job markets, whereas in larger metropolitan areas not so much. The reasoning is quite simple. Large multinational corporations, by and large, are located in dense populated urban areas, where the vast majority tend to use similar hiring practices. This often includes having candidates participate in an assessment center. Besides the obvious, what does an "assessment" actually entail?

Assessment centers are professional training centers designed for testing elite candidates. This can take place on or off corporate campuses due to a lack of space and for security purposes. They serve strictly to "measure" how candidates, with various personalities, assert themselves in real life work situations via a series of various tasks and scenarios.

Activities are designed for single and group

participation, all in an effort to measure "critical competencies" *matched* according to company desires. These can range from problem-solving exercises in a group setting; to one-on-one role- playing activities with corporate management. Many different parameters are recorded and judged along the way - opening the door to potential problems.

While it's impossible to predict with 100% certainty which core competencies management will be in search of, in all likelihood, the following items will be on that list: "communication skills"; "your ability to work within a team"; "leading or being lead"; "persuasiveness and influence"; and most importantly, "problem solving skills". Generally speaking, companies are in need of hiring because gaps are present and they need to be filled. A byproduct of this is why companies must test for various aptitudes. Venue plays an important role in testing for these abilities, let's dig deeper.

Venue:

Assessment centers can take place inside corporate offices or at outside agencies like recruiting firms. They can also be held inside a hotel – similarly to my assessment center involving 100 candidates, more on that later. Now let's address what an unsuspecting candidate might encounter.

Concerning company personnel, you could find yourself among a wide-range of employees conducting these forums including: managers, department heads of: social media, marketing, sales, logistics, accounting, and HR; or *recruiting* firms that will conduct the entire process from start to finish. In terms of measuring aptitudes, assessment centers are equipped at doing both a "group" or "individual analysis" or even both. In the event their hiring for an outside sales position, it's probable you'll participate in some individual tasks, like a role- playing exercise selling directly to a manager.

Whereas, if you were to interview to become a member of a project management team, it's feasible you will be given a group task to see how well you interact and perform among your peers. In both settings, critical skills will be measured along the way; based on particular group and individual assessment center "formats" detailed next.

Group Assessment:

This can include any number of candidates, though usually less than 10. The setting could take place in a boardroom; or an area where candidates are gathered around a table tasked with performing a team exercise. Such as a case study, debate, or survival test (example below – group activity). The actual number of "assessors" in the room can vary, but usually 2-3, plus a facilitator providing instructions to the candidates while other assessors take notes.

Upon entering the testing area, don't be alarmed if you happen to see a double-mirror in the room. These are sometimes present based on the job and skills sought after. Speaking of which, it's hard to say with any real certainty what those might be.

Below is a list of the many "critical-competencies" a candidate could be evaluated on; designated by a "plus" (+) or minus (-), depicting positive or negative behavior. The results of which will then be recorded on "tally-sheets" provided to all the assessors. Afterwards, the results will be compiled in order to make a final "assessment." Here's a list of potential competencies:

Teamwork

+ Who brings other people into the discussion

+ Who encourages other people's contributions

+ Who builds on and adapts others ideas

+ Who appropriately challenges people's views

+ Who volunteers to keep track of time / take notes

− Who talks too much

− Who is insensitive to the feeling of others
  Influence

+ Who helps shape the discussion and takes charge

+ Who keeps the discussion on track

+ Who ensures that everyone understands the objectives and whose points are accepted

− Whose arguments are ignored / talked over

Communication

+ Who listens before contributing

+ Who contributes consistently throughout the discussion

+ Who ensures that everyone understands the objectives and whose points are accepted

– Who is clear and concise throughout the discussion

– Who is very dominant – interrupting others' contributions

– Who does NO talking at all Problem Solving

+ Who uses the information provided effectively

+ Who provides creative solutions to the problems

– Who wanders from the subject or introduces unnecessary tasks

Commercial awareness

+ Who understands the business and nature of the industry

+ Who ensures that the suggestions and recommendations are appropriate for the business

+ Who understands the brief and sticks to it[17]

As you can see there are many *critical competencies* one can be judged on. Avoid the negative points and don't concern yourself about meeting all the positive ones, as this could hinder your performance in doing so, merely by attempting to satisfy a single requirement. Just be yourself and utilize the techniques provided in past chapters. Key recommendations to follow:

Assessment Center Recommendations:

Recall in Chapter 2 (group interviews) we spoke about the importance of acquiring everyone's first name "before" participating in the group activity? The significance of this recommendation will present itself as you begin directing your peers by their first names during the group task. The others will undoubtedly take notice of your initiative, and management also for that matter, positioning you as the candidate to beat.

Likewise – for me to provide you the full gamut of recommendations to use while being assessed, I must address two key critical competencies you must be aware of at all times: "Personal behavior" and "level of participation". These two will be scrutinized from the time you walk in till the time you leave. Receiving an invitation to an assessment center is a high honor and requires alike effort.

233

It will be your job to stand out for the right reasons by playing an active role and speaking out when necessary. Otherwise – all the hard work you will have put in may go to waste paving the way for management not to select you. Therefore, whatever you do, don't just sit there and remain silent. Take part by offering good sound answers using the other candidates in the room as your personal assistants. Let's take a closer look.

Leading vs. being lead:

One adage I learned early in my career: "Lead or get out of the way." The assessment center will be comprised of many candidates from various backgrounds, skill sets, and personalities. This is a breeding ground for others to easily walk all over you. It will be your responsibility for that not to happen.

By having an understanding on what to expect beforehand, and preparing for it, you will have the confidence going forward in performing at a high level. It won't be necessary in leading per se, but it will be in your best interest to play a role versus being a ghost in the room.

In other words - speak up and offer clear and concise

responses about the subject matter, so management will have "*data*" on you regarding the *competencies* above. The personalities in the room will vary - hence the reason you are there. If you aren't a natural born leader then let someone else fill that role. The *key* is to not let "everyone" in the room treat you like a doormat. It's your future that's on the line, you must fight for it.

So if you're uncomfortable leading a group, play the role of "deputy" and ride the sheriff's coattails to victory. Sometimes playing sheriff in this particular situation isn't the best strategy. To reiterate from earlier, you won't know the competencies or personality traits the assessors are in search of, but coming across as a boisterous arrogant narcissist will certainly be your undoing, and believe me this happens more times than none.

There will always be someone in the room who feels they need to express their opinion in order to be "heard." Don't be that person. If you don't have anything constructive to say remain quiet. Management will respect you more.

Influential vs. Aggression:

Aggression will get you nowhere in the corporate world. There is simply no room for hostility in the workplace, or anywhere for that matter. Work is what it is – work! No reason to make it any more demanding by creating undue stress. Considering multiple personalities will coexist in the room concurrently; in all likelihood – there'll be an overly aggressive candidate trying to make a good impression among them. Let them hang themselves.

Focus on being influential by gaining co-operation within the group by offering sound advice during the tasks. Half the people in the room will self- destruct just by being ghosts and overly aggressive. That leaves the other half, which is where you want to be. Influential over aggression will win out virtually every time. How to accomplish this? By *involving* others! This will accumulate major points in the plus column with your assessors. I'll explain.

Getting involved:

Having many divergent temperaments in the room, all vying to make a good impression, may discourage you from participating. Don't allow that to happen. On the contrary

– envision the other candidates as stepping stones for your eventual success in securing the job.

Use caution when applying yourself during the tasks and try not to be someone you're not. Get involved at a time suitable for you, but do get involved! Otherwise, the assessors will not have a reason to hire you. There are 3 ways you can do this:

1st: Facilitate or be the leader of the group.

2nd: Be the presenter.

3rd: Be the time-keeper.

Considering option three – this doesn't mean if you were to volunteer to be time- keeper that you only sit and keep time. Quite the opposite – besides agreeing to this undertaking, it would be wise to involve yourself in other ways, like interjecting pertinent information to the group whenever feasible. The relevance is that volunteering sends a message you are interested in playing an active role within the group, versus just sitting on your hands.

The difficulty is in choosing the *right* moment when to jump in without being perceived as an instigator. Another way of getting noticed, surely to gain the attention of the assessors is by "involving" other group members.

How? acquiring everyone's name ahead of time, now you can facilitate the conversation by asking the others in the room for their opinion. For instance - "I believe we should do A, B, C... what are your thoughts on that 'Susan'?" Another way is to include those who haven't contributed *anything*.

For example - maybe one of the more shyer candidates, who hasn't uttered a word all day, has a solid point to make about the topic, and through your leadership are able to pull it out of them, like so: "I agree with what you're saying 'George', however let's see what 'Lucy' has to say as we haven't heard from her yet."

This will go a long way in demonstrating your "awareness" of what's happening around the room, including what others are saying. By offering their involvement would set the stage for a more meaningful group session through embracing everyone's ideas - not just a select few.

Furthermore, by displaying your ability to cut in at

appropriate times will signal to assessors an ability to keep the conversation flowing in a positive direction. Having said that, one thing to keep in mind going forward is, never feel pressure in having to play a role you're uncomfortable with.

In fact, playing the role of leader can sometimes be risky. The facilitator of the group will have most of the *spotlight* on them, which could backfire as a result of them being seen as too overbearing. Why is this important? Because teams inside companies could already have good leadership in place, and by bringing in an overzealous new hire, the potential may arise that this person could clash with existing team members.

In closing, the take home message is to not feel pressure into playing a role that isn't suitable for you, but to play "a" role - nevertheless. One role that needs no introduction is the role of *acknowledging* - which we'll cover now.

Acknowledge:

I can't emphasize enough the importance this one simple trait has on everyday life. Acknowledging is just common sense and symbolic of one showing *respect* towards others. It validates you are aware of your audience and that you are paying them attention.

Another aspect is that it confirms you share a common interest in solving the problem at hand by listening to all inputs - *regardless* of source. So whenever another candidate within the group is talking, you should be looking in their general direction, nodding your head up and down in agreement, or side to side in disagreement.

Whatever the case may be, prepare yourself for the need in articulating a response if and when the baton is passed to you. If that were to occur, deliver your response in a calm, yet confident manner, using short and concise sentences to stay on point.

Smile and Remain Positive:

The process of interviewing can be daunting for both candidates and hiring managers, as the responsibility lies within management to find the most suitable people to fill voids within their organizations. This is magnified to the nth degree during an assessment center.

Often at times, this can involve testing you in ways never having thought of, providing moments of personal frustration and self-pity; causing some to lose their cool, showing their disgust as a result. This type of behavior would obviously be viewed negatively and most certainly gain the attention of hiring managers. You may now be thinking, "What does this have to do with me, and why even bring this up?"

All points well taken, however, it's important to shed light on how interviewers could deem a candidate undesirable, causing them to be weeded out in the process. Negativity plays an extremely important role in this, especially during the final "selection" process. Even the most positive person can fall victim (at times) to doing something out of character, unknowingly; potentially painting them in a bad light. The reason it matters?

Projecting negativity can easily link one to being a *"gossiper"* – which is precisely the point. Displaying any negative behavior could label you as such and multinational companies frown heavily upon this. Allow me to share with you how you could be judged adversely in the following paragraphs, before the assessment (or interview) ever takes place.

"Gossiping" within corporations is a contributing

factor to *inefficiency*. Having others express their disdain about another team member behind closed doors makes for a toxic environment that will grow like cancer until it's removed. Let's face it, people of various backgrounds may not see eye to eye at times, but when at work, it's important to put aside differences and complete the task at hand.

This is the reason why companies have "team-building" activities. They don't always work, but often times they do. *Productivity* is the main objective and an increase in such will likely yield higher profits, leading to bonuses in your pocket. Wouldn't that be nice!?! So it behooves one to remain positive, yet on the other hand, realistic in the same sense.

"Smiling" too much can equally be just as bad, so do it appropriately according to the situation. Lastly, some key points to be cognizant of regarding "attitude and behavior", before participating in an assessment center.

Upon arriving early to your assessment (or interview), if you notice that something isn't right within the setting, try not to get caught up in displaying any *negative* behavior about it. I realize this is common sense, but you would be surprised at how many candidates have actually blown

242

interviews before ever taking place. A little reminder, cameras are everywhere you look these days so assume you're being watched at every turn. Therefore, the moment you step foot out of the car, leave your personal baggage inside and put your happy face on.

As you enter the building you may encounter some obstacles, testing you *emotionally* in a manner that could put you in a negative frame of mind. No matter the situation don't go there! Don't show any negative reaction of any kind. This means if one of the elevator cars is shut down, forcing you to wait an exorbitant amount of time, don't get mad and repeatedly press the "up" button over and over.

Another example could be that the coffee machine isn't working properly. Forget about it, you're not there for the coffee anyway. Yet another could be the water cooler. Maybe it too is out of order. Not your concern, remain calm and go about your day. And *most* importantly, upon meeting the other candidates – absolutely positively do not under any circumstances gossip about anything, especially the others, nor show any negative sentiment, whatsoever.

Maybe the traffic was bad coming in, doesn't matter; maybe the parking attendant was a jerk to you, doesn't matter; maybe the receptionist spent 5 minutes texting her boyfriend while you stood watching and waiting, doesn't matter. You get the point. At the end of the day, *none of it matters*, you are there for one specific purpose and that is to outshine all others in order to get the job. Let's help with that by turning our attention on what you might see during a group activity within an assessment center.

Below is an activity characteristic of a "group task" one might see while participating in an assessment center. The number of applicants during this activity would involve 4-8 people

Group Exercise Task:

"You're returning back from a holiday in South America and your shuttle flight to the airport is forced to make an emergency landing in a small clearing in the Brazilian rainforest. You, the pilot, and your fellow passengers have sustained only minor injuries, but the plane has broken into pieces and the communication equipment has been destroyed on impact.

Before crashing, the pilot had reported a problem with one of the engines, so there is a good chance the authorities will start looking for you after you fail to arrive at your destination. However, the forest is very dense and it will take days to reach the edge of it by foot. You cannot remain where you are as the airplane fuel will catch fire. Upon searching the wreckage and remains of the suitcases you find the following items:

1. A guide to South American plant species

2. 3 elasticated luggage straps

3. 6 frozen airline meals

4. 4 blankets from the plane

5. A pack of 24 anti-malaria tablets

6. A 3-meter square piece of opaque plastic sheeting

7. Tourist map of Brazil

8. 2 large bottles of factor 12 sunscreen

9. Mobile phone with GPS, fully charged

10. 1 liter bottle of the local alcoholic spirit

11. 3 boxes of chocolate chip cookies

12. 4 current paperback novels

13. First aid box

14. Compass

15. Flare gun with one flare

16. A Swiss Army knife

17. A book of matches from the hotel

> You are unable to carry more than 7 items from this list. Items containing more than one object still count as one item." You have 20 minutes to reach your conclusion and present back to the assessors.[18]

In regards to this example, there is no "correct" answer as one could argue a case for most, if not all of the items. In spite of this – the assessors will be watching how you interact among each other with a particular interest on how the group will render a decision on the final 7 items. Although a number of competencies could be on the list for judgment, don't concern yourself with trying to determine them.

Remember to get involved by choosing one of the 3 roles as discussed earlier and just be yourself. Interject and smile when appropriate without coming across as being overbearing or fake, plus acknowledge the others upon them speaking. Above is a typical example on what you might encounter during a "group" activity. Below is an activity a candidate could come across in either a "group or an individual assessment":

Combination Group | Individual Task

First task would include candidates (in this case - 6) seated around a table with a panel of 3 managers sitting side by side facing the candidates. The task could be debating one-on-one against another candidate regarding a highly controversial issue such as "capital punishment" or "mandatory vaccinations." The panel will determine the topic and which side (argument) each candidate will deliberate. This could result in you having to debate against your own beliefs.

My recommendation is to remain calm, jot down 3 points for the basis of your argument and present them in a composed manner, while allowing the other candidate time to rebut. As their doing so, respect their answers by nodding your head up and down "acknowledging" you are listening and then articulate one of your 3 points in defense.

247

Try not to get into a "heated" discussion. Your assessors are measuring your "tone of voice" and watching how you present yourself in the course of a *stressful* situation. Avoid pointing any fingers or jamming your finger down on the table while presenting one of your 3 points. Lastly, a good way to end is by saying, "We can agree to disagree and I look forward in discussing this further at a later time."

Afterwards, your performance will be judged and the decision will be made whether or not to advance you to the next round. Most times candidates will move forward, but occasionally a select few will not for various reasons. This could range from a candidate not articulating their argument in a confident manner, or by losing their composure while debating with another candidate. As for the remaining candidates, they will move on to the "individual" task - involving a single panel member to conduct a face-to-face interview.

This could take place in the same room, or in a separate break-out room. Depending on the job opening, the task will involve testing you on a desired skill-set. For example, if the open position is for a sales job, then the task could involve the candidate role-playing a sales-call with one of the mangers. The performance will be measured against the others; afterwards - the original panel members will come together and formulate a decision which best suits them and the company.

　　　It's important to disclose the example above could also exist during a regular group or panel interview as detailed in Chapter 2. Let's now take a look at the "individual assessment" center and how it might overlap within the group format. After that, I'll present a personal account of my assessment center involving 100 candidates in Philadelphia, PA.

Individual Assessment:

Just to be clear, "overlap" between the two formats is quite common. Many assessment centers lump *both* formats under one umbrella, but it's important to distinguish the difference between them. In the group format, critical competencies of each candidate will be measured based on interactions with "other" group members; whereas with individual formats, one-on-one tasks are used to measure distinct abilities besides deficiencies within the individual. It will depend on the job

249

offering on which type will be assigned.

On the other hand, expect any job using a *consultative* approach; such as in software sales, medical sales, sales manager; or any other type consultant to use a mixture of both formats with a particular emphasis on "individual" performance. In other words – you will be "judged" on how well you perform *individually* in front of a manager.

For instance: role-playing a sales-call with only you and a manager. It should also be noted that upon entering an assessment center, you may be among a large number of candidates to whom you could perform tasks with or without. Therefore, though you may be in the same room with 50 other candidates, it could be categorized as an "individual" assessment if you were there only to perform *singular* tasks involving a manager. Much of it will depend on company needs.

In particular – the number of positions the company is need of hiring for. Plus, whether or not it's just for one job opening, or to hire an entire sales-force, never assume anything. Even if many candidates are congregating inside an assessment center; as you all, theoretically, could get the job. The best way for me to drive this point home is by detailing my personal experience inside an assessment center while at Astra (now-AstraZeneca).

My Personal Assessment-Center Story:

Would it surprise you by the time of my invite to the assessment center in Philadelphia (one of three) that over 10,000 resumes had been received and sorted through? And, out of those 10,000, only 300 candidates received an invitation to the assessment center? To take it one step further, from those 300, only 100 were offered jobs, *contingent* on passing a drug test and background check (see Chapter 10).

In retrospect, securing the job at Astra was one of the pinnacle moments of my career as a consultative sells professional. Had I not worked there, much of this book could never have been written. I'm extremely grateful for the time spent there. Let's provide you all the details.

Since I lived on the East Coast (Charleston, SC) I was slated for the Philadelphia assessment center. The other two in San Francisco & Chicago. The assessment lasted one full day, but all the participants were flown in the night before. Upon checking in (Marriott), I was informed I would receive a packet the following morning and to be present in the grand ball room at 8 am sharp.

The room accommodations were pleasant with each of us sharing a double room. My roommate joined me from a nearby town in Columbia, SC (capital of S.C.). From the onset - Steve and I hit it off, conversing all night about what to expect the following morning. We arrived on time and sat together at one of the 50 (two-top) tables. The meeting had kicked off with a congratulatory welcome speech on being selected as the finalist to compete.

Individual packets were then handed out, consisting of a personality test with 30 minutes to complete. Afterwards, we were asked to write an essay why we wanted to work for Astra, receiving an additional 30 minutes to do so. Following that we were asked to pull out the remaining papers inside the packet, which consisted of product information about their anesthesia products.

Our task was to role-play a sales call with a physician and a separate sales call with a pharmacist. A schedule of role-play times and room numbers were provided allowing 90 minutes for preparation. Steve and I spent the time preparing back in our room. One item was lidocaine

(Xylocaine) – a short acting anesthetic and the other – a long(er) acting anesthetic - bupivacaine (Marcaine). We had to sell the benefits of one over the other. After a few minutes time, it was easy to determine the longer-acting product offered "significant" benefits over the shorter acting one – less applications in particular.

During my preparation, I noticed Steve creating charts displaying the differences between the two meds. He offered them to me and explained it would be a good idea to use them as a "sales-aid" during our mock sales calls. At the time of this assessment center, I had never had any "formal" sales training, and thought it couldn't hurt to try. I copied his graphs and proceeded with my note- taking. Shortly thereafter - I left to do my role-plays.

Individual Role-Plays:

Upon entering the (guest hotel) room, I noticed two men in suits, one sitting and the other standing in the corner. I thought this was a bid odd; nevertheless - the show must go on, right? The gentleman who greeted me was George Roadman, former VP within the company, and I don't recall the other guy. George wasted no time just said: "ignore the guy in the corner and I could start at any time."

No small talk, strictly business.

For a professional who built their career on making small talk and building rapport, this man would have none of it. I began asking him questions about his current usage of Xylocaine vs. Marcaine; with an understanding that their product portfolio consisted of a long-acting beta-blocker for blood pressure control. George didn't make this role-play any easier with his belligerent behavior and condescending body language.

Turns out his grandfather was former president of Georgetown University, and to make matters worse, he was also accused in having a major role in the infamous sexual harassment scandal discussed earlier – "Abuse of Power" (Chapter 5). Looking back on it now, it all made sense regarding his arrogance. Nonetheless – I continued with the call knowing I had to "close" him; failing to do so would result in my failure in getting the job.

We were allotted only 10 minutes and after being shut down for most of it (by design), I displayed the graphs Steve had assisted me with and stated my reasons why he would benefit more from using the longer-acting med. After he became a bit more responsive, I then tried closing him multiple ways, but he wouldn't budge an inch. I then asked for another meeting 2-weeks later, his response: "I'll think about it."

The sales-call had ended and I felt the job ended with it from not having gained any commitment from him. I later learned it was all part of the game as management had been instructed not to give-in and allow anyone to "close" them. Their reasoning was to see how far we would take it. I recall Roadman stating to me: "OK, OK, time's up," in a comical way which gave me a glimmer of hope.

Next came the pharmacy call, similar in nature, but with different managers. Though the premise of the call was a bit different, the interviewers were more receptive and friendly - "thankfully" so. The goal of this call was simply to sell the pharmacist on *"stocking"* their shelves, for the sake of availability once a physician prescribes the medicine. So the selling strategy was a bit different, nonetheless much less stressful than the first call.

To sum up the call – I presented the bar graphs and asked them to bring in a few bottles, as the physicians in the area had responded positively to my earlier presentations. The interviewer responded with a few objections; specifically - cost and side effect profiles followed by him saying he would think about it. I tried a few more times, and then gained agreement for him to "consider it,"

I felt a bit better, but still dejected not having closed him, but still better than the first meeting with George, who apparently had an axe to grind. The individual role-plays were now in the books, but the individual *assessment* was far from over.

We were practically research study material as we were scrutinized in everything we did, including every meal we ate; breakfast and lunch, plus one last cocktail party that brought the assessment to a close. What could they possibly judge us on while eating? To find out, one must consider the location of their headquarters – which was located in Sweden. This meant stark differences in mannerisms as compared to America.

The obvious being the holding of silverware. Europeans nearly eat everything with their knife and fork, including open faced sandwiches. Aside from this - we were also being monitored on how we conducted ourselves in the presence of others, including: restaurant staff, managers,

256

and the other candidates.

It became abundantly clear that every move and word we made and said was being observed. I recall some candidates speaking openly how they were still recovering from the previous night due to drinking too much. I *never* saw them again. I also recall management continually asking how the assessment was going for me personally. I took that as a sign - I too would never be seen again if I portrayed any "negativity."

Thus – my reasoning for presenting you all these "details"; so you won't make silly mistakes like *complaining* or staying out too late the night before your assessment. To conclude – I'll share the particulars about the cocktail party and how new-hires were selected.

Final Event – Cocktail Party:

It had been quite a long and exhausting day already, but the most important event (little did we know) was yet to come. The cock-tail party was every bit as important in becoming a new hire as one would think. One would need to read the article in Business Week (Chapter 5) to gain a complete understanding as to why the "cock-tail" party was such an integral part of the hiring process.

To be clear – you will never encounter this in any assessment center for a job interview – but I feel the need to include this because of the *"networking"* element it imposes and how vitally important this is. I'll explain.

After both the individual (sales call) role-plays, I had planned to "pack it in" for the night due to an early flight out the next morning. That is until one of the mangers approached me and said for me to *"make an appearance"* at the cock- tail party before turning in. How could one refuse, right?

Judging by the level of supervision that was on display throughout the course of this assessment, I was on high alert not to endanger the performances I had put in earlier. And so, I limited myself to one beer during the party *nursing* it for nearly an hour. Some might say why drink at all, which is a reasonable question; however, as a moderate drinker, I did not want to be the topic of discussion about whether or not I drank alcohol.

Nowadays there's a *plethora* of non-alcoholic beverages on the market, not so back then. Upon my arrival, a manger pulled me aside and said, "Whatever you do make sure you 'meet' everyone in *this* room." I was a bit surprised at this, but grateful nonetheless as this turned out to be one of the determining factors for being hired. Upon entering the room, I ordered a beer and was asked if I wanted a glass, which I replied: "yes, please."

Come to find out – Europeans mainly drink alcohol (in all forms) from a glass, rather than a bottle, and this was one more aspect of our assessment we were being judged on. I typically like drinking from a bottle, but felt compelled to follow the managers' leads (all) drinking from their glasses. "When in Rome...."

Afterwards, I took credence to what the manager had told me earlier and began "working the room" introducing myself to the others and spending no more than 5 minutes with each of them. I can't tell you what the other candidates were doing during this time, because I was so focused on making it around the room. I just acquainted myself with as many managers as I could, expressing how delighted I was to be there.

Most mangers responded by asking me how I felt about my performance. My answer was the same for each, "It was tougher than I expected – but I prepared well and did the best I could." Shortly thereafter - a few extended the party to a nearby bar – which I felt was off limits given the situation. In consideration of this, allow me to share a few important factors worth mentioning:

It's important to never let your guard down during the interview process, including at an assessment center. Some of the candidates at the cock-tail party ordered one drink after another and smoked like freight trains. I don't condemn smoking, as my mother had done so for 30 plus years (it was vogue back then); but – use caution in doing so as you never know what might become of it.

If you see a manager smoking and you're asked to light up with them, then it's your call. Building rapport and finding commonality will increase your chances of getting the job, so it may be to your advantage in taking them up on it. Whatever you do – don't order more than one drink – period!

Looking around the room it was obvious who the real alcoholics were, as most of them had fixated themselves in one corner of the room and never moved away from that spot. Needless to say – I never saw them again either. Play it cool by making an appearance and blending in with the others, while not standing out to the point of being sent home. One additional note about why you should always "work the room."

> ❖ "Working the room" is a critical essential in determining a candidate's worthiness in a social setting. Consequently - by working the room (introducing oneself to others) can be the difference between getting the job or not. The next morning after we had flown home, the managers stayed behind in order to compare notes on us.

How New-Hires Were Chosen:

My manager later explained the entire process to me from top to bottom. He said an A4 size photograph of each candidate was placed against the wall and each manager (about 15) gave their feedback. Much of it was based on the individual role-plays and other "personal interactions" during breakfast, lunch, and the cock-tail party. Upon hearing this information; I thought to myself, had I not made an effort to speak with the managers "in some capacity," then my chances of being hired would have been dire.

Having said that, I was extremely fortunate to have been contacted by the manager (beforehand) advising me on what to do; otherwise - the results may have been different. While it's highly probable you will not encounter a "cocktail" experience such as the one described above, my goal in sharing it is to provide you with as many "actual" interview scenarios as possible, so there will be no *surprises* for you.

In closing, about a week later I got the call from the recruiter and offered the position after a long 6-week process involving over 10,000 resumes; 2 – phone screenings; 3 face-to-face interviews; and an assessment center involving 100 candidates. It was by far one of the hardest experiences in interviewing I had ever encountered; and looking back in remembrance, it was certainly worth it considering my career success there, and the life lessons learned in the process.

The next item on the agenda is to detail the process which occurs "after" management has offered you the position. It is worth noting – that just because the job has been offered to you, there are still some final hoops that one must jump through before the job is "official."

Chapter 10

FINAL HURDLES

A congratulatory note is in order here, but it's still a bit premature before one can celebrate. Everything you've read thus far is knowledge you can take and apply in your pursuit to gain meaningful employment. On the other hand – not to be a bearer of bad news, especially having traveled this far through the maze, but the party cannot commence until after being *cleared* to work. The best way to explain it is to compare it to professional sports.

In sports, whenever an athlete is traded from one team to another, it's *contingent* upon passing a detailed "physical" before the trade can be honored. In the corporate world, this corresponds to having a background check, though (metaphorically), this will not be your average physical. In fact, you'll be confronted with more tests behind the scenes than one could possibly imagine - hence the "final hurdles."

In failing to meet a threshold within these test

264

parameters could be grounds for *rescinding* your employment contract (offer). Consequently, the following words are what a candidate might here upon receiving a job offer: "We are extended you an offer for job (X) *'contingent'* upon passing a *'background'* check."

The main scope of this chapter is to provide you a deep understanding to what occurs behind the scenes when companies perform these "full" background checks. For many, this will be an eye-popping education, while others may already have knowledge in this area having found out the hard way as I did.

So it's crucial to fully immerse yourself in understanding the ramifications that can result from not taking the following items seriously: Job and personal references; credit check, social media activity; drug testing and possibly others. The vast majority of which will be nearly impossible to modify in the short-run.

Nevertheless, despite the fact you'll be powerless at making meaningful changes in the short-run, significant changes can only be sought after having accurate knowledge on the precise measures one can take in correcting reasons for losing job offers. Let's begin the

265

tutorial starting with "follow up."

Follow – up:

In every aspect of business, proper follow up is essential for maintaining client relationships. Should interviewing be any different? I think not, being that this is an indispensible area which must be accounted for. Likewise – following up is as elementary as it gets, yet many drop the ball by not doing it, thus the reason for reiterating its importance.

So here's the general rule; if you've accepted a business card from a manager or any associate within the organization, you should send an immediate follow- up email after conclusion of the interview. An exception: speaking to a single person within a group, yet receiving three different business cards.

In that case, I would "CC" all of them on the email and mention their names in the body of the email. It can't hurt. The more people you can influence through following up, the better your chances for them to remember you when it counts. In addition to the email – I'd send a handwritten letter as well. Why?

Because it exhibits a *personal* touch as very few receive

handwritten letters these days. It validates a sense of going the extra mile by taking the time to write the note, address the envelope, and mail it versus sending an effortless email. It will definitely score you bonus points in the end, and could even be the difference maker when it's all said and done.

References – Personal & Work:

Two types of references exist: Personal and Work. These often overlap where your work reference could be personal and vice-versa. Personal references are not commonly used for individuals with a great deal of work experience. Generally – candidates with many years of work experience will rely on their work references instead.

Personal references, on the other hand, are mainly used for entry-level positions and those graduating from college or university. It's a chance for employers to get a feel for whom they might be hiring by contacting the personal reference in question. "Personal" doesn't mean mother or father; it means someone close to you who could vouch you would be a good employee for the company. Some of the questions asked during a "personal" reference check:

- "How long have you known Kevin and tell me how you first met?"

- "Is there any reason you feel Kevin would not be able to perform this job at a high level?

- "Could you provide some reasons why I should hire him?"

These are just a few of the questions you could be asked. Generally – 2 to 3 questions will be asked to complement information already obtained in your interviews. Therefore, list a friend who knows you pretty well, plus who would never say anything negative about you. To add, make your "reference" aware of your recent employment history, so the both of you will be in tune with one another. Let's move on to work references.

Work References:

Work references are self-explanatory to where candidates will have to provide a name and number of previous employers. In particular, a former manager over you, or possibly even a work colleague that can speak on behalf of your performance. In the end, the HR department of your new employer will contact your previous employer's HR to determine work dates and positions held within said company.

Furthermore – it would behoove you to have a couple of different managers in various work roles; who will agree to a direct phone-call, or write a recommendation letter for you to include in your war-book. On the other hand, let me explain why checking work references can be a danger to some.

If in fact you had left your previous employer on bad terms, this information could permanently be displayed in your employment file. The formal language used to document your file would be whether or not you're *"eligible as a rehire"* or not. Thanks to (US) federal labor laws protecting citizen rights, HR departments are limited as to what they can and cannot say.

Let's say you're hired on the contingency of passing the background and reference check. It's customary for HR departments to call your previous company and simply ask: "Is Kevin eligible for rehire?" The company's response should *only* be a simple "yes" or "no." A follow-up question could ensue if the answer were "no." However – your previous employer is swimming in treacherous waters if they choose to elaborate with a lengthy response and by doing so, could potentially cost you the new position you worked so hard to get. While it may be legal, it would be illegal to ask specifics like: "Did Kevin get along with his work-mates?" Keep this in mind when changing jobs.

The take home message above is not to "burn any bridges" when leaving one company for another, because the time you will have put in will ultimately be lost. No matter the reason for your displeasure, you should try to leave on "good terms," meaning to "bite your tongue" and move on.

Therefore, if any of the following were to occur: narcissistic and psychotic managers, unreasonable sales goals, complete incompetence within support staff, slave wages, management by fear, outsourcing your jobs to foreign workers, or others; take the high road by keeping negative thoughts to yourself and use every employer as a *springboard* for securing a better job. This will enable you to utilize your talents elsewhere, giving others an opportunity to appreciate you for who you are.

In defense of those who may have experienced this. I'm no saint in this area either, as I've burned a bridge or two after displaying my disgust working within some companies. Reflecting back – very little was gained from me venting my frustrations (expressed in written notices to leave company X). Also, once you do burn that bridge, you can no longer rely on them to be an advocate for you in the future.

Considering how important social media is nowadays with the likes of LinkedIn, it's critically important to maintain as many working connections as you can. Taking this into account, even though you may want to lash out verbally or through written form, think before you do. Let's share the reasons why companies perform drug tests and criminal checks - besides the obvious.

Criminal Record Check:

This is standard by all multinational companies to ensure there aren't any major convictions or pending litigation against you, such as a DWI conviction, hindering you from performing a job, like having to drive a company van (truck) or car. In this particular instance, if one were convicted of this, the courts may establish certain parameters for you to operate a vehicle, but this isn't guaranteed. Most (if not all) companies will pass on you if they happen to find a DWI on your record.

A criminal record check can easily be obtained upon the signing of your application. In a nut shell, if you have a felony conviction, your chances of being hired into a white-collar job are almost zero. Felony, by definition, is a crime punishable by more than one year in prison. But, in certain cases if the conviction was for a "non-violent" crime — such as selling a large amount of marijuana — then it's possible to have the conviction "expunged" (removed from public record) after serving your sentence.

Misdemeanors can also be expunged after paying a fine or serving out the sentence (less than one-year). Typical misdemeanors include: petty theft, public intoxication, disorderly conduct, trespassing, reckless driving, vandalism (graffiti on walls), and prostitution. It depends on the type of job you're applying for, but having a misdemeanor on your record, would inevitably paint you as an *irresponsible* person. So my best advice is to be *upfront* with your employer and state the reason why it happened. Next up, types of drug testing you could face.

Drug Test:

After receiving a job offer and accepting, before starting your first day you'll have to pass a drug test. This is due to many factors: protection from potential loss of productivity; companies wanting to maintain a drug free workplace; protection for other co-workers; and to limit potential litigation down the road if an employee were to cause an accident while on drugs. No use on providing statistics as to the specific impacts "drug use" can cause at the workplace. The effects are real and challenges do arise upon their use, from work accidents to absenteeism.

It's become standard practice nowadays to just to test everyone from the CEO, down to the stock clerk. The type of drug test - in terms of specific drugs tested - will depend on the job position and industry. For example: if seeking employment within the medical sector, expect a more rigorous exam, including the testing of prescription opioids. On the other hand, selling pest control may only require a urine test, seeking the use of cocaine and marijuana. The various testing methods below can be used alone or in conjunction with others to test frequency of usage.

Hair & Body Hair:

This is the ultimate test in determining casual or frequent drug use, because drugs embed themselves into the hair follicle after each occurrence leaving behind a roadmap of their use. It can also determine the specific drug taken as long as that specific drug is being tested for. And while it's possible to trick a urine test, it's virtually impossible to *"cheat"* a hair test due to the inability of "diluting" it. Regular hair tests can determine drug use up to 90 days - whereas body hair can extend that figure out to potentially 6 months or more.

However, at least an inch and a half of hair is necessary for a viable sample to detect back 90 days. So if one were to take a longer sample of hair, it's technically conceivable to test further back than 90 days, but this generally applies to law enforcement like FBI, DOD, Homeland Security, and others. So don't worry in the event you may have smoked a few joints while in college a year ago. The purpose is to look at your *recent* behavior. The actual test is quick and painless.

Hair is taking directly from the root and the remainder is discarded (unless law enforcement); if a candidate is bald, a sample can be taken from underneath the armpit or from body hair. No hair sample can be taken if the candidate is completely shaven from head to toe. That said, samples attained are placed in small plastic bags and sent to testing facilities yielding results within 10 days.

Blood & Saliva:

These tests (specifically blood) are designed to detect *immediate* drug use in the body such as alcohol, cocaine, methamphetamines, opioids and others. A blood test can detect the type of drug use and amount, but is limited to a shorter detection window; whereas saliva can range from a couple of hours up to 2-3 days. The reason for its frequent use is due to its non-invasive nature and speed of extraction. Moreover, it's relatively cheap compared to other testing methods.

Urine:

Most likely you'll have this test in conjunction with another. It's by far the most common due to being first on the block. It's become the standard for drug-tests throughout the world for its simplicity and the fact you can "freeze" the samples, plus can test them whenever you please. Urine tests are expressed in number of "panels" — one panel representing a particular drug.

For example, if I say the candidate received a "5-panel" urine test - it means their sample was sent to the lab and tested for 5 different drugs, for instance: alcohol, cocaine, marijuana, amphetamines, and maybe PCI (or angel dust); compare that to a "10-panel" test which could test for: cocaine, methamphetamines, amphetamines, opiates, THC, barbiturates, benzodiazepines, methadone, methaqualone, and propoxyphene.

There are also 4, 5, 6, 7, 10 and even 12 panel tests dependent on: corporate culture; job responsibilities; safety concerns within the work place; potential for drug abuse within the company; and so on. The bottom line is you won't know what you're being tested for unless they tell you at the lab. The test can generally detect drug use for the past 7 days, but cannot determine *frequency*.

If you are regular drug user and have used within the past 7 days, then you have reason to be worried. If not, but recently smoked marijuana within the past 7 days, it may or may not be detected. Can it be cheated? I don't have a definitive answer one way or the other, but promoters argue yes; through "dilution", "substitution", and "adulteration." You can decide for yourself by researching this often debated topic. Let's now turn our attention to a heated topic of discussion many candidates take for granted, their personal credit status.

Candidate Credit-Check:

Many younger candidates may be surprised to hear that their credit reports will be examined by the same company (outsourced to another firm) hiring them. Yes this is true! This is a hotly contested issue and has spurred much debate on the *validity* of conducting such tests in the screening of applicants. Adversaries argue that it amounts to *discrimination*, whereas advocates maintain it's an important tool for employers in guaranteeing the quality of new employees.

For the record – I've personally been a victim of this practice that cost me a few job offers – of which, I took full responsibility and the necessary steps in resolving. Yet, despite everything, without having faced these temporary set- backs, much of what you're about to read could never have been written.

In fact – had I been privileged to this ensuing information before partaking in risky undertakings – less dire outcomes (personally) may have occurred. In consideration – let's now provide some particulars by taking a deep dive into this controversial topic, starting with addressing the top "5-reasons" why employers use this method for screening candidates. Afterwards, I'll share two personal interview stories how credit-status negatively impacted me.

The top 5-reasons why employers use them can be summed up beautifully in the testimony of Michael Aamodt - an expert and Ph.D. of DCI Consulting Group, Inc. - working on behalf of the EEOC (Equal Employment Opportunity Commission). Dr. Aamodt provided personal testimony regarding the *validity* of credit checks in determining the impact (if any) they have on "work performance". Here's part of the transcript:

"On the basis of surveys conducted by the Society for Human Resource Management (SHRM, 2010), approximately 60% of organizations use credit checks when selecting employees for some jobs. Given this high degree of use, it is fair to conclude that many employers believe that credit checks provide useful information for certain jobs. From my discussions with employers, there are five common reasons why organizations use credit checks for employment purposes:

1. The organization is required by an external agency (e.g., a bonding company, a state government) to conduct credit checks. Thus, the employer is not using the credit check as a means to predict performance, but instead, as a means to fulfill a requirement by the bonding agency.

2. To reduce potential legal liability due to negligent hiring.

3. A belief that employees who are in financial distress might have an increased likelihood to steal or accept bribes. This is a common reason stated by law enforcement agencies for why they include a credit check as part of a comprehensive background investigation. I am not aware of any research on this topic that would support or refute this belief.

4. A bad credit history suggests that the applicant is irresponsible and is not conscientious and thus will

279

be a bad employee. Employers relying on this belief are in essence, using a credit check to replace or enhance a personality inventory.

5. Employees with financial problems will be stressed due to the financial burden and thus will perform more poorly at work. There is some empirical support for this argument as meta-analyses have demonstrated statistically significant, but small, relationships between stress and work performance (p = -.13; Podsakoff, LePine, and LePine, 2007) and stress and organizational citizenship behaviors (p = -.16; Chang, Johnson, and Yang, 2007). There has also been research demonstrating that employees under financial stress have lessened job satisfaction (Bailey, Woodiel, Turner, and Young, 1998) and are more likely to miss work and spend work time trying to solve financial problems than are employees without such stress (Bagwell and Kim, 2003; Kim and Garman, 2004; Kim, Sorhaindo, and Garman, 2006).

Given this thinking, the question becomes: Are any of these reasons valid? Although there is considerable research that supports the use of credit scores in making consumer decisions, "there is little research exploring the implications of using credit checks in employment decisions."[19]

Based on the above – we can see there is a *need* for more research in determining a *causal* relationship between credit reports and work performance. Considering how this personally impacted me in the way that it did, the practice of checking personal credit reports as a screening tool should be "banned" until *sufficient* studies are conducted demonstrating validity. This is further illustrated based on comments by Eric Rosenberg - director of state government relations for TransUnion (one of the big 3 credit reporting agencies in the U.S.; Equifax and Experian representing the others):

"At this point, we don't have any research to show any statistical correlation between what's in somebody's credit report and their job performance of their likelihood to commit fraud," (Oregon State Legislative Hearing – January 12, 2010)[20]

Banning the practice of using personal credit reports to establish job performance would be prudent, but not logical, given the fact profits would suffer from the big 3 credit-reporting agencies (TransUnion, Equifax, and Experian); which I believe to be among the most "hated" and powerful organizations in the U.S. in their ability to lobby politicians in Washington, D.C.

Speaking of which; Equifax – recently responsible for one of America's largest data breaches ever – was just voted "the most hated" company in America as of the completion of this book.[21] With that in mind – if it doesn't impact lawmakers personally – as in the case with New York State Assemblyman Michael Benjamin[22]; then the majority of citizens' voices impacted (minorities including African-Americans) may fall on deaf ears.

That is, unless of course, their constitutional rights (as citizens) are negatively challenged, as in the Department of Labor case (decision) in 2010, which ruled against Bank of America; resulting in a $2.2 million judgment for discriminatory practices related to credit checks concerning African-Americans.[23]

Notwithstanding, the fact remains the battle will rage on between corporate titans and lawmakers; for the purposes of going to bat for their constituents to be in their good graces come election time. Despite this, however, progress continues to move forward in a positive direction from a candidate's perspective; there are laws in place allowing for credit checks with exceptions. These are dependent on each state and generally fall under the following exemptions:

- Managerial positions;

- Law enforcement positions;

- Positions required by "law";

- Positions involving use of a company/corporate credit card;

- Positions coming in contact with more than $5000.

You can see where most "white collar" jobs would fall into one of the exemption categories. Sadly, while laws have been enacted to help job applicants in recent years, the fact is these credit-checks will continue to be a driving force in determining whether a person is employable or not.

One thing to make clear; the credit-report is just one *mitigating* factor in a host of other determinants; however, if your credit-report is *damaging* in a way that paints you irresponsibly, this will be nearly impossible for you to overcome. Mindful of this – many ask if their "credit scores" are also part of the report; thankfully – no.

Presently, only financial information regarding past and present obligations is analyzed. Many reading this will say how can this be "legal"? Aren't I required to give my *"authorization"* for the company to view my personal information? Great question! The short answer – Yes! After completing all the steps necessary to secure the job, you will be asked to fill out an application to include your job details from your resume.

You're hired, but first must go through certain formalities for HR to create an employee number, set you up for training, corporate card, and possibly a company car, among other things. At the bottom of every application (U.S.) you'll notice a *section* next to the signature box providing "full authorization" for the company to conduct a "full" background check upon signing.

This is where you *sign* away all you rights. Once they have your signature, it's free reign to investigate you in ways you've never thought of; including, but not limited to: pulling a credit-report, driving record, criminal record, social media activity, and so on. Don't despair if your credit is less than stellar, we'll talk about things you can do to address this. But in the meantime, let's look at some other reasons why credit reports are pulled.

Credit reports can shed light on financial woes resulting from risky business adventures going belly-up; to ill-fated events, like a divorce or medical catastrophe. Regardless of nature – it can determine whether you're wallowing in debt at the present, or recovering from financial ruin based on a past event. In other words, it can identify exactly what your current financial status is (now) at a *specific* moment in time, besides displaying a sense of how *responsible* you are in paying your debtors.

If the company were to check your report and find many "charge-offs" (defaults on your debt); then red-flags may appear as to your ability in performing said job requirements, causing a backlash of sorts within HR departments. Indeed, having delinquencies will inevitably label you as a "risk" to hire, and HR will either block you from being hired (happened to me once), or leave the decision solely up to the manager liable for you (a second occurrence).

For me personally – I had to succumb to this *stigma* after months of fighting it – which did cost me a few job offers described above. But in the end, I wound up stronger and wiser as a result, upon restoring what was in need of repairing. Which, in this case, were blemishes on my credit report from risky investments gone awry. I was young and foolish; not to mention – filled with greed. Nonetheless, I owned up to the mistakes I had made, settled with all the banks involved, and paid every single one of them back, mending my credit-status along the way.

A humbling experience much to my chagrin; yet, on the other hand, a silver- lining was discovered in the process after uncovering a treasure-trove of information, which led (in a large part) to the writing of this book. Speaking of which, the two personal interview stories making up the basis of this chapter, will be available for you to read below. But first, I want to briefly explain a couple of other reasons why employers check credit, which will make my personal stories that much clearer on why credit-status has such an impact.

Other Reasons for Checking Credit:

Blemishes on a credit report can also hinder a candidate

from being approved for a corporate credit card, which perhaps may block them from receiving a job offer as well. By not possessing a corporate credit card could be problematic when having to pay for luncheons and entertainment while dining out with customers.

The reason being, multi-national corporations are required to have transparency within their accounting departments in order to appease their shareholders. Accordingly – all expenditures are usually paid and settled via use of a "corporate credit card" in order to have a "paper-trail."

If you were to use your own personal credit card, this could cause problems with filling out your expense report, because many companies integrate credit card charges directly into their CRM systems for streamlining paperwork efficiency. Less paperwork (theoretically) results in higher productivity. A potential productivity killer would be the result of theft or embezzlement within a corporation – hence the reason for wanting transparency.

This is yet another important reason why companies will shy away from candidates with *questionable* credit. Put yourself in the position of a small business owner needing

287

to hire for a managerial position, requiring the handling of daily cash. Upon doing a background check you see the candidate, who has won you over, owes $50,000 in credit card debt and recently opened up a second mortgage on their house, plus is 3 months late on the payment. What would you do?

How would you react? Would you hire them anyway? What if the primary reason you're looking for a new manager in the first place is because the *last* manager stole from you. Considering this, one can see why the business owner may choose to pass on this particular candidate.

On the other hand, background checks are *expensive* and many small business owners won't spend the money on them. But this isn't a concern within multi- national companies. Given the same scenario above, it's clear why management would have reservations on hiring this individual. It's possible the candidate could be approved for a corporate credit card, but the realism of their financial situation could also tempt them to use it for personal gain that could damage a company unless bonded.

Such cases could include: deliberately over quoting travel expenses to extract more money than entitled to;

buying personal gifts while on corporate business, paying for fuel, personal automotive repairs; charging expensive luncheons and dinners with family members and recording them as a customer outing. These are just a few instances and there are many more, but it's not just relegated to the little guy.

Controllers and CEO's (with perfect credit) can be some of the worst offenders of this fraudulent behavior. Many documented stories exist where use of company funds for personal gains among executives drove their own companies into bankruptcy – namely Bernie Madoff. In fact, my former CEO (Lars Bildman - Astra) was indicted for embezzlement a few years after the sexual harassment scandal first broke for expensing $1.5 million in home improvements on the company's dime. One thing's clear, the use of credit reports for determining employment isn't going anywhere.

Having said that – it's of my opinion the sole candidate remaining at the end of a treacherous interview process should be allowed to explain themselves as to why their credit is the way it is. Otherwise, a grand opportunity to hire (hypothetically) a top-producer eager to redeem themselves could be lost as you'll discover in my personal interview stories to follow.

The first is about a gutless manager, who upended me, for fear of being terminated himself, on account of his own bad decision making. The second is about the longest interview I ever endured. In fact – it wouldn't surprise me if it were listed in the Guinness Book of World Records for the longest interview to ever have taken place. And if you're wondering, I did check, but could find no such category. Without further ado:

Medicis Pharmaceuticals (now – Valeant)

Having worked in the medical field for the bulk of my young professional life, Medicis seemed like the operative fit for getting my life back on track again, having risked nearly everything at a chance for securing financial freedom. Considering my expertise in the health-care industry and the success I enjoyed there, the job as a territory manager position within their Southeast division was just the thing the Dr. ordered for me to resurrect my career.

John phoned me up after noticing a local (Charlotte,

NC) phone number on my resume, even though my medical experience had been worked back in Florida. Being a newly hired manager of the Southeastern region, John was in desperate need of help within the Florida market as their numbers were atrocious, and he saw me as a viable prospect towards fixing that.

Our first meeting was held in a diner; where it was apparent from the start, his eagerness at learning all I knew about the Florida market, to determine if I was the right fit for the job. Actually, I had vast experience within the dermatology market in Northern Florida (Orlando to Jacksonville) and could definitely help John "right the ship."

In addition, I was quite keen on returning back to Florida to "right my wrongs" – and grateful this opportunity had presented itself in assisting with that. The fact is, I really enjoyed living in Florida; it was my life, and I can see myself eventually living out the rest of my days there.

The interview itself was pretty laid back like 2 friends talking. I was asked the usual; why I left each job, and if I had a do over, would I "change" anything. Although this was a trap question, I wasn't concerned in the slightest. Truth be told, I still felt as if no matter what I did, I'd still be his front-runner, given my connections in Florida.

Likewise, my answer to this particular question has always been the same and still remains that way: "Hindsight is 20/20 and you can't look back, one can only look forward and given the situation, I made what I felt was the best decision for me at that time and must stand by it." All the same – I didn't change it for this occasion either.

In retrospect – do I have "regrets?" Hell yes! But it's of my opinion to keep these things to oneself, above all, during an interview. That said, some candidates will no doubt have more baggage than others; so, if you're in the group with more, it's best to take the "high road" and leave your past where it belongs, in the past!

The manager will (hopefully) see you have learned from a devastating situation and have put your best foot forward in rebuilding. If it's apparent you haven't put it behind you, then one may think your mindset isn't where it needs to be, likely giving another candidate the nod.

The bottom line - I knew I was his prime candidate -

but he had 2 others to interview (company-policy) before extending me an offer. He contacted me a week later to meet up again, and upon doing so was holding an application in his hand. I had already prepared my defense on what to say, before completing what essentially would be a useless application. All the pain and anguish began to rush to my forehead, as my failed business ventures (once again) were about to come under scrutiny.

In the past, we had touched on it, but not to the level that a "credit-check" would render me unemployable. Yet, I knew. I knew all too well what was about to take place; as he began explaining the need for me to complete the application, in order to be considered for employment.

In other words, he was hiring me for the position, "contingent upon passing a background check." I agreed and then offered up a little more transparency into what his HR department might come across while viewing my report, some of which they may not be able to "overlook."

He seemed perplexed; as I simultaneously admitted to having lost a recent financial advisor position over this. He assured "everything" would be fine, though he began to view me as a pariah. Based on his response, I knew he had never encountered such a situation, plus the fact he was about to receive an "education" – on account of being a fairly new manager. To my demise, I knew (in the long run) this would be a free tutorial, preparing him for similar situations in the future.

In comparison to the financial advisor position I had just lost within UBS; due to imperfections on my credit report; *the catalyst of which, led to my discovery of all this information.* I knew the ultimate decision awaiting me with this particular job, and the weight of it all was becoming too much for me to bear.

On one hand, I needed work in order to begin the process of rebuilding my life; whereas, the single reason for not gaining work was due to blemishes on my credit, which could take years to fix, further exacerbating the issue. How could one possibly overcome this? How would any HR department approve a candidate based on this? A few days later John called and stated HR had completed their background check and that he was thankful for my honesty in giving him a heads-up about my personal situation.

Then what John said next completely *flabbergasted* me, by expressing the fact HR *had left the hiring decision up to him!*

294

Internally, I was elated, because I knew how Florida was single-handedly killing his regional numbers, and how I could remedy that fairly quickly upon my hire. In my mind, I had already begun the process of thinking where I would live back in Florida.

Then reality struck as John uttered: "Kevin, while you're clearly more qualified than the other candidates, I cannot take another risk on hiring you at this time." I was a bit confused by this statement, by the fact he had said "another." I asked him to clarify; confident I could persuade him otherwise, and still believed the job was mine, regardless.

He said, "My first hire in the Florida market did not work out so well; and if I were to repeat that, 'my' job would be the one in jeopardy." I couldn't believe what I was hearing. On one hand, I was the one guy who could plug the gaping hole causing him not to sleep at night, yet on the other, was being refused the opportunity in doing so because of "his" fear of making another hiring mistake based on a credit report.

I was floored, yet – again! Though I didn't give up hope and tried persuading him to reconsider, it just wasn't in the

295

cards. As I documented the last interview results; sadly, it now dawned on me how credit-status was every bit as important as the interview itself.

Longest Interview Experience – Ever!

The formal name of the open position was a – "Service Sales Representative" (SSR). My resume was an easy match based on having learned SPIN Selling Skills, and the working knowledge I had of their operation from my tenure selling chemicals. The recruiter called immediately upon me responding to their job advertisement and promptly scheduled me for a phone screening. It lasted a total of 15-20 minutes and covered the usual. Then a few days later – I had a second phone screening with HR asking me virtually the same questions (worded differently) and why I wanted to work for Cintas.

Pondering the question why I wanted to work for Cintas was mentally debilitating, as I was still in the process of purging the loss incurred regarding the Medicis position. The truth of the matter was my mind was still thinking of Florida. So transitioning back to my hometown (Charlotte) in need of securing work, after some odd number of years upon graduating University, wasn't going to be easy.

Having spent nearly 10 years in Florida and for me to close that chapter to start anew was proving far more difficult than expected. That said - I knew what was at stake interviewing with Cintas; a good salary ($40-50k), car allowance; full benefits package, including a matching 401-k plan. This would give me the shot in the arm I so desperately needed.

The pressure to find a well-paying job was mounting and the longer I went without one, the more difficult it would be securing one. So I pressed on, reviewing previous notes, while spending a great deal of time pre-planning responses to behavioral questions, in anticipation of being asked about my job history. One week later it all paid off.

I'm no psychic; on the other hand, my intuition was dead-on in my belief that Cintas would use a "structured interview" utilizing S.T.A.R. How I gathered that? From the fact they trained their sales force in SPIN selling as did Astra. So it was reasonable in assuming a possible correlation between both companies. One thing to keep in mind when interviewing with large multi-national companies; most of them have similar hiring practices; what works well with one usually works well with another.

In fact, many of them hire the same consultancy groups experienced in selling expensive HR modules; designed to cover all aspects of the employee onboarding process - including the training of staff members on how to interview candidates. So making that connection was extremely helpful.

My initial face-to-face interview began with Lori, who would ultimately reside over me. She was similar in age as me and wasted no time on small talk. It became clear I was one of many she would be interviewing that day having bumped into the next candidate on my way out.

The interview started out like most, asking me the particulars on my resume and my responses included all the techniques described in the book. She then asked why Cintas, which ended up being a home-run question for me, because I had previously sold chemicals to Cintas in my first ever sales job.

From that moment on I knew I had the job. Afterwards - I played more of a consultative role than a candidate by sharing detailed information about the cleaning process of their uniforms; and how that might impact business if their finished product (essentially – clothes) weren't up to standards.

Lastly, I sold her on the fact how I could easily transfer this knowledge against their direct competitors Aramark and Rental Uniform Services. Based on all indications from her body-language, I seemed to be pushing all the right buttons.

The remainder of the interview was a breeze and afterwards, she asked if I had time to complete an online questionnaire (lasting 30 minutes), in addition to interviewing with their service manager. I took this as a positive sign as I seemed to be moving through the process at a faster rate than normal, though I had no clue what the entire process would entail.

Having interviewed with the "service manager" – I followed suit with the General Manager (GM) one week later. The structure in the way they both conducted the interviews was much the same as Lori had done prior, by probing me with different behavioral questions. Each of them liked the fact I had previously sold to Cintas.

The rest of the interview process would follow as such: a full day field-ride with one of their sales representatives, then a follow up discussion with the hiring manager (Lori), followed by an interview with the Regional VP, and one last (third) meeting with the hiring manager. After acing the internal interviews with both the service manager and GM, they scheduled me for the ride-along with Mark a few days later.

After joining up with Mark, we drove for the next hour en route to his territory on the outskirts of Charlotte. He was a nice guy in his mid-20's and I was about 10 years his senior. So career wise – I was light-years ahead of him mentally – but financially was on the outside looking in. Just 3 years prior, I was training and mentoring guys like him on a daily basis. He would soon discover this upon me coming to his aid during his last sales call.

Before that moment, however, he had asked several pointed questions about me and my sales experience. It was as if he was reading from a "script." He had no idea at how skilled I was at the very game he was playing, but I had no choice, but to play along. Most of the day was spent servicing "existing" accounts and making a few cold calls, which then led to his last "planned" call of the day; thankfully - as I was a bit tired of being asked the same questions from previous interviews.

I recall him being a bit jovial ahead of the call; this opportunity would have landed him a decent gain to his incremental income, not to mention stealing business away from a competitor. For me, that was the exciting part. On the other hand, little did he know I was an expert (literally) on the cleaning of clothes from my former career selling businesses like Cintas. This was further enhanced by having the "lingo" and the ability to articulate it with Mark's client. The customer was a Utility Power Company using "Aramark" (Cintas' #1 competitor) in a position to change as their contract was up for renewal. A pleasant woman approached and took us to the boardroom where 5 other employees were awaiting our arrival. Mark clearly had good rapport with her and I was simply introduced as a "guest" riding with him.

The meeting was scheduled to last for an hour. Upon the start of the meeting, we all shook hands and the woman introduced everyone and stated the basis for the meeting. Mark then began asking several "close-ended" questions – following the SPIN protocol. She answered them faithfully.

For those not versed in using SPIN, the whole premise behind it is to discover a "problem" and then turn it into a "bigger" problem. For the purpose of eliciting a response from the customer — in order for them to realize a need to take action. It works to perfection if done in a non-confrontational manner, in other words, as if you were having a casual conversation. Mark was not at that level just yet; though much to the credit of Cintas — he did know the process.

Mark then moved into this area of the strategic selling process by asking the woman some "problem" questions about their current arrangement. This led to an incredible opportunity to paint the competition in a negatively light, but the issue wasn't with the question, or the answer for that matter, but with Mark yielding a "silent" response. He initially asked, "If there was anything you could change for the better, what would it be?"

A great question with the answer being — "We have a problem with "staining" on our uniforms and our present company cannot seem to solve it." Mark seemed puzzled by this, because it wasn't a standard cost or "service" issue, but more related to cleaning quality — which was my sweet spot. Having noticed many of the members present in the room beginning to lose faith in Mark solving their problem, I stepped in and took over the call by "implicating" the problem Mark had uncovered; by asking them a series of question tailored to the "staining" issue. This led to the discovery of more "negative" information.

For starters, their employees had to wear the same uniform multiple times due to their spares having to be rewashed, because of the staining issue, resulting in having to spend more money on new uniforms. This in turn led to morale issues within their work-force and eventually chaos for their HR department. I remember asking the perfect follow-up question as Mark sat with his eyes wide- open with a blank stare:

"How would a company – who could provide a "stain" formula tailored to your employees' work environment – resulting in cleaner uniforms be of benefit to you?" The woman looked at the other members with excitement and said (I kid you not) – "How long would the process take for my guys to receive their uniforms if we signed up today"? I let Mark takeover from there, because I had no earthly idea! But, you wouldn't have known that based on

303

their reaction. In fact, upon our departure, the woman asked for my business card and I remember grabbing one from Mark and jotting down my number, handing it to her in response.

All the frustrations from recent disappointments had subsided; at least for that moment, helped in part to what I considered a small victory; a sense of accomplishment if you will. As we walked towards Mark's car, I felt right at home again in offering up some sales tutorials while on the job. Not only for Mark, but for two other reasons: the prospect of getting the job, and more importantly – my psyche. I needed a win, and needed it badly. Today was a "win-win" for the both of us.

Upon getting into the car, he had a look of shock upon his face and actually "thanked" me for stepping in. Surprising to some, I admit I wasn't too comfortable in doing so, but my "instinct" from training just took over, and I just rolled with it for better or for worse.

In spite of everything – Lori called during our way back into town and asked about the day. He spoke about the call, pointing out how I had assisted during the process, which set me up nicely for the follow-up interview - 2 days later.

Mark wished me good luck and felt confident the next time he'd see me would be working for Cintas. The grueling boot camp continues; next up – follow up interview.

Follow-Up Interview (surprise - surprise):

The following week, I met up with Lori again and we both knew I'd be her next hire, but the Regional VP was still standing in my way. Despite this, I took nothing for granted and remained on my A-game. Knowing full well how easily problems can occur at the most inopportune time by taking one's hands off the wheel. This time was no different and before meeting up with him, Lori had asked about the specifics of the ride-along after hearing how "productive" it was.

So I recapped with no mention of helping out Mark during the sales-call. I just stated how delighted I was to have had the opportunity to spend the day with Mark. She acknowledged and then much to my surprise, revisited earlier questions from the previous 3 interviews I had had with the other managers. So for about the first 10 minutes, it was as if I was speaking to my best friend – then bam! Kevin, better focus or you're outta here.

I guess the biggest surprise for me was the fact that it was totally "unexpected." I was ready for more questions, but was blindsided by being asked the same questions previously (by the 2 other managers), yet in a different way. This is why I have emphasized throughout the book on keeping an "interview journal" for this very reason.

Fortunately, I had detailed notes on all the previous interviews, I just had to ensure I kept my answers consistent; otherwise, I could fall into the trap of telling two managers, asking the same question, two "different" results. This would ultimately keep me from getting the job, without ever knowing the reason why. Remember those words? A little reminder: "We've decided to go a step in a different direction." In other words – you screwed up, but we won't tell you the reason. Good luck finding it.

Regardless, I focused on providing exactly the same answer (word for word) as before, during prior interviews. With every consistent answer being uttered from my mouth, she demonstrated more positive body language, confirming my answers were in-line with what she had on her questionnaire. This line of questioning lasted for 30 minutes and then she informed me I would have "one" more interview with the regional VP; and lucky for me - he would be in town the following week for a conference - saving me a trip up to Cincinnati.

I met with (Dave) the VP at 10 am for only 30 minutes, though I was scheduled for an hour. He was very direct and to the point. He took one look at my resume and asked, *"I see you have experience in SPIN selling, how would you rate your effectiveness as a sales representative?"*

Being asked a question like this "opens" the door to many possibilities for a candidate to either come across as too arrogant or too weak. VP's care about results, without them, they'll also be looking for a job. So I stayed within the confinements of my resume by stating, "My effectiveness can only be measured by my results," and then I identified specifics within each sales job and how I was able to accomplish this. His only other question: *"Why Cintas?"*

I explained my previous work history had prepared me for Cintas and that Cintas had an environment to where I could flourish if given the chance. I recall him smiling at me as if I definitely had the job, then said there were other candidates needing to be interviewed before a final decision could be rendered.

Afterwards – he asked if I had any questions, which I followed by asking the money question. His response: *"Be happy you've made it 'thus' far."* He then firmly shook my hand, wearing a slight grin, and said Lori would follow up with me soon. I took that as a good sign, but was perplexed about his last comment to me – hence probably the reason he said it. The marathon continues with the last interview, followed by the "talk."

Last Interview:

Three days later - Lori called and asked to meet for lunch near her office the following week. I was confident I had the job, but still couldn't celebrate as of yet. I vividly recall her positive body language upon meeting her at the restaurant. Despite that – I was heavily on guard as I hadn't signed anything and wasn't taking any chances. Then, as I was coaching my inner-self to remain calm, she pulled out an application form, simultaneously extending her hand and said: *"Welcome to the team!"*

The taste of victory this time around was sweeter than ever, considering the exhausting process having just been through. I recall looking up at the ceiling thanking God for a long and hard fought battle, which ended up consuming the better part of 6 weeks. "Internally" – I was overjoyed with emotion, yet held it all in. I was proud of what I had accomplished and knew in my heart I had done everything in my control to secure this job, now came the part I couldn't control and my worry began to creep back in.

The Discussion:

As Lori and I ate our lunch and basked in a celebratory victory glass of wine, the big question for me was not when, but "if" I should break the news to her about my "financial situation", or should I just roll the dice and let the chips fall where they may. I knew the answer already, as the one thing I could "control" was being open and honest about the situation. The glass of wine was beginning to sour as my conscience had informed me the party was now over and the real "selling" must commence. So as I was finishing up the application, I came down to the signature box and noticed the same "disclaimer" upon signing that read: "By signing your name, you give Cintas authorization to do a full background check, including blah, blah, blah. Here we go again, how do I break this to her.

✦ Mental note:

> Whenever you open yourself up by doling out
> negative things about your private life, most
> people will frown upon hearing anything negative
> and will begin to look at you in a different light.
> Their mannerisms will completely change. It's as
> if you had just told your girlfriend, you had
> cheated on her with her best friend. Sorry to be the
> bearer of bad news, but it's virtually impossible to
> recover from, once you open up that can of
> worms.

The same applies within the employment world and unfortunately, this was something I was all too familiar with. Being "blacklisted" for taking a risk shouldn't blackball a person for the rest of their life, but within many multi- national companies, this is indeed the case until you can "clean" up your mess (whatever that may be); and Cintas was no different.

This now begs the question: Should I keep to myself and say nothing? Or, act in a manner as with all my previous situations by telling the truth? I stand by what I said earlier in regards to the importance of being open and honest. As they say: *"The Truth Shall Set You Free."* In this case, it truly did!

The End - Thankfully:

So as I enjoyed the feeling of becoming a soon-to-be productive member of society while being selected as a new team member within Cintas, albeit only for just a brief moment, it was time for me to spill the beans and endure the pain. The pain of watching the transformation of what would have been my future manager turn "executioner."

One week later and no sign of Lori; the recruiter called and said, get this: *"They decided to go a step in a different direction."* So after enduring 6-long weeks of interviewing involving 9-total meetings for an "entry-level" sales position; Cintas moved on, and with that, so did I. It's called life in the big city and life goes on.

Roll with it or get rolled over. Cintas did me a favor by rescinding the offer, leaving me "sunnier" days ahead. Shortly thereafter – I secured a job in advertising sales within the automotive sector; where I set multiple sales records and thrived for years, eventually landing me top sales honors, and a regional trainer position.

In closing – If you're aware of your credit status (most people are) and believe it may endanger your ability to pass the background check, then it's better to be upfront and discuss it with your point of contact "before" they perform the background check. Don't take any chances in believing a bad report will be dismissed by HR, because it won't. However – by being upfront about it there's a chance they'll accept it and hire you. Let's now close out the chapter by offering up some credit-reporting tips and an explanation of what "bonding" is in the following paragraphs.

Credit-Reporting Tips

If you know for a fact your credit report could put you in danger of losing a job that is no *fault* of your own (stolen identity). You can provide a "statement" - in 100 words or less - to the credit reporting agencies. By law, the agencies must include this statement on your report.

For instance: If you are recently divorced and notice a loan on your credit report that is in default; agreed to be paid by your ex-spouse, describe the situation in 100 words or less and provide supporting facts as to the validity of your claim. This will provide "your side" of the story as to the reason why there is a default on your personal report.

❖ Note: Use caution when writing this statement as it cannot be *deleted or edited!*

In addition to adding a statement, tracking your credit status on a *continuous* basis is equally important in maintaining financial integrity. Even if no changes were to occur, periodically checking your reports against identity theft is exercising prudence. By doing so, your chances of having an unauthorized line of credit opened using your information would be limited.

This occurred with a close friend, taking nearly 6 months to clear up. If this were to happen while seeking employment, theoretically, it could cost you a job or two without you ever knowing it, until it's too late. So do yourself a favor and check it regularly. One last reason for checking a candidate's credit is to determine whether they are bondable or not.

Bonding:

What is it? An insurance policy protecting a company (whose bonded) against one of their own (employees) from incurring a financial loss due to theft, negligence, or other various reasons. It's in essence a "personal work" policy.

This is the sole reason for a background check. It's to see if you are in fact, bondable, given your past. So if you have a criminal record, a felony or major driving offense, you may not be bondable. For example:

Let's say you're applying for a job requiring the use of a company car. If it's revealed in the background check that you have a DWI on your record, you would be deemed *ineligible* for the job. Without having the ability to "drive a vehicle," you wouldn't be able to perform the job responsibilities – thus "couldn't" be offered the job.

Another instance would be if a candidate had robbed a bank (5 years ago) and was "convicted" – revealing a felony violation. This information would remain permanently on their record, including a credit report; due to the seriousness of the crime in nature. Therefore, the likelihood of ever being approved by a bonding company would be extremely low.

The latter example seems a bit harsh, but there are candidates who dabble in recreational drugs like marijuana, unaware of the consequences from exceeding weight limits for simple possession (misdemeanor). And in the event those limits were exceeded, a simple misdemeanor could result in law-enforcement upgrading it to a felony, eventually landing the new charge on the candidate's credit report.

State laws vary with respect to the amounts (expressed in weight); nonetheless, if you're a recreational user, don't fall into the trap of believing by having "no record" will hide the fact you use it sparingly. A *"hair test"* can determine precisely the number of times you've done so in recent past.

Summary:

The background check can be a killer to many. Indeed, but now since you have the knowledge of what it entails, you can now begin the process of correcting what needs to be fixed. At the beginning of the chapter, we mentioned "following-up" with your interviewers and how.

We also spoke about the differences between personal and work "references." By "personal" – I don't mean mother or father, but someone else close to you, besides a family member who can speak about your character. Work references, on the other hand, should be a former manager that can articulate the value you would add to your new employer.

We then shed light on criminal record checks and drug testing. Explained was how a felony would ruin any possibility for gaining work within a multinational company. Also, we clarified the need to remind recreational drug users of the fact that the practice of doing so can now be detected very easily by a random hair test.

Next, I detailed definitively how credit-status can impact one's career with two personal stories serving as proof. Plus, how checking a candidate's credit- report is now an integral part of the background check, besides the importance of checking one's own credit. Likewise, if any barriers to employment appear evident, the need to clean them up in the quickest way possible is key.

I provided a legal way for stating reasons for having questionable credit; by providing the bureaus a statement of "100 words or less" and having it included on the report. I explained the caution in doing so, as this statement cannot be altered or deleted. We touched on bonding and the reasons for not being "employable"; if in fact, you aren't bondable.

Lastly, one further impediment in need of explaining will be the focus of our next chapter. Alarming in many ways, the practice of employers examining the activity of candidates' social media accounts. Candidate, beware!

Chapter 11

SOCIAL MEDIA

Social media is yet, another "obstacle" one must overcome during an employer background check. This is a relatively new phenomenon that didn't exist a generation ago, but now, more than ever, companies are placing a premium on its validity for basing hiring decisions. On one hand, it's an incredible tool for connecting friends and family; on the other, it can be detrimental towards one's career if its deficiencies aren't kept in check. Some interesting facts about its history, before touching on its shortcomings.

Before "social-media" was ever designated a term; a pint-sized online networking site – unbeknownst to the world – named *"Six Degrees"* launched in May of 1997 by Andrew Weinreich, connecting friends and family via "user profiles."

Social media has evolved into a phenomenon ever since, spawning a tech revolution resembling the likes of the 1940's industrial (U.S.) revolution. It has helped create mega wealth for a select few with the advent of Facebook, Instagram, Twitter, Snapchat among others. And with advances in smartphone technology, social media has become a dominant form of communication, leaving behind traditional forms in place of more faster digital options.

With Facebook's Messenger; WhatsApp; Instagram; and a relative newcomer in Snapchat; "Millennials" have ditched the conventional talk feature on smartphones, in favor of using ones' fingers texting. In fact: a 2014 Gallup poll confirmed text messaging now outranks phone calls as the dominant form of communication among Millennials. A full 68% of 18 to 29 year-olds say they texted *"a lot"*, dipping to 47% among 30 to 49 year-olds and 26% for 50 to 64 year-olds.[24]

One thing gathered from this is that people are using their eyes and fingers more than their ears and mouths; thus - leading to an ever increasing demand for online content serving Millennial appetites. *"Content is king"* in the lucrative world of SEO. It's the raw material necessary for driving the engine of the social media train. The *only* industry in the world where the mega rich – like Mark Zuckerburg pay zilch for "raw materials." Incredible – isn't it?

Imagine owning a business where the cost of raw materials were free! The point is very simple. What would Zuckerburg do if the masses suddenly stopped providing these raw materials – by not posting content on Facebook? Interesting question isn't it? You may be thinking, *"What difference does it make?"* Social media is used practically by everyone and is here to stay.

True, but the main point is the fact your *"privacy's"* at risk for the entire world to see. I don't mean your credit cards or banking information. I'm referring to your *"actual"* privacy. In other words - daily activities spent with close friends and family making up your real "private-life." Let's take that one step further. What if I were to tell you more than 75% of employers and recruiters look at social media profiles to gain insight for making better hiring decisions? Surprising? If not, it should at least gain your attention.

The good news is that you can *lock* down your Facebook settings where only your closest friends can view this activity. The bad news is, nowadays many online *media* sites require you to log in via Facebook. Which means you won't be able to voice your opinion, *anonymously*, when it comes

320

to posting a comment on a controversial article printed "online." An exception being the use of a fake Facebook account - which Facebook has really cracked down on with the presence of so much "fake-news." They now require a mobile number upon signing up.

In spite of this – many *unsuspecting* users post frequently without setting up any privacy measures, having no real concerns of the consequences for employers to view their private activity. To add, Facebook is encouraging, through email notifications and other means, its users to share posts and videos of virtually every experience in one's life. So if by chance someone were to "tag" you in a post or video, employers could view this publicly as well. So keep this in mind when tagging and posting content on Facebook; as a questionable post could come back and haunt you during the background check. Let's move on.

Another social media platform that has gained a great deal of attention in recent memory, with help from the political spectrum, is Twitter. Oh how I love Twitter. For me personally, I've never used it, but someday I may, in order to extend the reach of my readers, but only when proper "safeguards" are in place. For now, I'll stick to the sidelines, as so many careers have been dashed within seconds after acts of "tweet-rage."

Heck, our own President uses it like a pacifier, to satisfy his daily agenda of antagonistic tweeting. A book could literally be written on his tweeting alone. And each and every morning upon firing off another round, somewhere in this world Jack Dorsey and company are laughing all the way to the bank for the free daily publicity.

Consequently - is it any coincidence that the character amount per tweet has doubled from 140 to 280 on November 7, 2017 - almost one year to the day after the election? I think not, as on the "actual" day of the election, Twitter pumped out and astounding 40 million election-related tweets - cementing its relevance among its 300 plus million users. Despite this - its shortcomings can be linked to misuse - as you will soon discover among celebrities and corporations alike.

Its challenges lie within the fact that tweets are never "purged." Unless you, the user does so personally, before a questionable tweet goes "viral" or gets "buried" (among the billions daily); opening the door for an old tweet to be dug up years later and used against you. With this social media

322

platform, your past truly does follow you for everyone to see, with a just a simple click of the mouse through Google.

So if you have a night out on the town with a little too much to drink and decide to tweet out an opinionated rant about what have you, then you too could be at risk for twitterverse turning you into an infamous celebrity before ever realizing it. Let's now turn our attention on how these internal safeguards, or lack thereof, have wreaked havoc within the corporate ranks, followed by some infamous Tweets from celebrities falling victim to it; beginning with one of my former employers in US Airways (now American Airlines).

US Airways:

- US Airways (now American Airlines) gets top vote for the most epic Twitter debacle in history by a corporation, by tweeting a response to an angry customer named "Elle" which read:

- @ellerafter: "We welcome feedback, Elle. If your travel is complete, you can detail it here for review and follow-up"; pic.twitter.com/vbeYgCuG25 – The photo (not pictured) in the latter code is a damaging pornographic image of a female lying on her back with a model 777 airplane inserted into her vagina.

- The tweet was taken down as quickly as possible, but not before many followers received it and re-tweeted. The company's formal response:

- US Airways @US Airways: "We apologize for an inappropriate image recently shared as a link in one of our responses. We have removed the tweet and are investigating.07:26 PM - 14 Apr 2014"[25]

- Rumor has it, a rogue employee working for an IT company, outsourced by US Airways, uploaded the disgusting image (tweet) in an attempt to sabotage the company, possibly to cause a drop in the stock price. Who knows, but shortly thereafter American Airlines bought them out. Coincidence? That's for you to ponder.

Aflac Insurance - Comedian - Gilbert Gottfried:

- ☐ Who's Gilbert Gottfried? Exactly! No – really; he's the "former" spokesman and voice of the famous

"Aflac-duck." He was also relieved of his duties after tweeting insensitive remarks about the "tsunami in Japan" uttering shortly after it happened:

☐ "Japan is really advanced. They don't go to the beach. The beach comes to them."[26]

From the corporate world to the lucrative world of entertainment, celebrities run amuck on Twitter daily. Some just can't get enough of it, while others use it as a platform to vent their dirty laundry. Ultimately causing public relation fire- storms resulting in tabloid behemoths like *"TMZ."*

Frustrations at times can boil over during heated discussions causing celebrities to quit this social media form altogether. As such the case with a former Hollywood A-lister in Alec Baldwin. Conversely, there are others who have followed suit, but only for a brief stint, as the vast majority re-opened their accounts soon after, including Mr. Baldwin. The following celebrity tweets will definitely bring to mind moments of: "What were you thinking"? Have a look:

Amanda Bynes and Rihanna:

o Amanda Bynes took Twitter to a whole new level with a seemingly unwarranted attack on pop star Rihanna and Chrissy Teigen of Sports Illustrated – Fame, calling both stars, "ugly." In one particularly notable moment, the former child star suggested Chris Brown's 2009 abuse of Rihanna was a result of her being, "not pretty enough."[27]

Rihanna and Chris Brown:

- This back and forth drama spilling over to Twitter should be no surprise after Brown's felony assault charge on Rihanna back in 2009 with Rihanna tweeting: "If I drop all my hoes for you and we still don't work out you owe me some hoes."

- Brown's reply: "She's not mine if she's everybody else's."[28]

Kanye West:

☐ Tweeted: "BILL COSBY INNOCENT!!!!!!!!!

☐ Kanye saying something controversial? I know, hard to believe. But even for Kanye, making a tweet saying Bill Cosby was innocent was kind of beyond the pale. People came down hard on Kanye, even other celebs. I mean it's one thing to support someone, but declaring him innocent? A lot has changed in 2017, and hopefully people are more aware that it's important to listen to victims." [29]

☐ Cosby Update: April 26th, 2018; a jury found Cosby guilty on three counts of felony aggravated indecent assault (sexual assault) and will likely serve up to 10 years in federal prison. He is 80 years old.

Josh Groban:

■ Tweeted: "Any time one of the greatest voices of my generation lip syncs an angel loses its wings."

■ His tweet was referencing Mariah Carey's disastrous New Year's Eve debacle at Times Square in 2016, where numerous technical glitches and failures occurred in the midst of her lip-syncing. He quickly deleted it, after suffering a bit of backlash, and apologizing profusely. [30]

Skrillex:

• Tweeted: "I wish I was aloud (sic) to use the N-word

sometimes (in a non-racist way of course)

- Yes, probably most of you caught the misspelling, but this tweet overall was a "super-dumb one."[31]

Alec Baldwin and George Stark:

o During James Gandolfini's funeral, George Stark (British journalist – Daily Mail) accused Alec Baldwin's wife – "Hilaria" of tweeting during the funeral incensing Alec to contest the allegations in a series of tweets accusing the journalist of not only lying but questioning his sexuality with gay slurs - which he later apologized for. A few of his testy tweets:

o "Someone wrote that my wife was tweeting at a funeral. Hey. That's not true. But I'm gonna tweet at your funeral."

o "George Stark, you lying little b---h. I am gonna find you, you toxic little queen, and I'm gonna f@*% you up."

Alec Baldwin continues:

o "How much of this s--- are people supposed to

take? With these f---king blatant lies EVERY DAY,"

o My wife DID NOT use her phone, in any capacity, at our friend's funeral. Now, f--k this twitter + good luck to all of you who know the truth."[32]

So, before I leave you with the *ultimate* "life-altering" tweet; Maybe the last comment from Alec Baldwin above should encourage you, too, to say "F—k" Twitter and leave it for those who want to play Russian Roulette with their career. Speaking of careers, let's see how a senior director blew one up - causing a worldwide Twitter chain-reaction - in all of 11 hours with just 170 Twitter followers,

The Infamous Tweet Heard Round The World:

Who can ever forget the *racist* tweet of "Justine Sacco"; launching the entire Twitter universe into a frenzy heard round the world - costing her job *"mid- flight"* in route to visit family in South Africa. As she made the journey from New York to South Africa, to visit family during the holidays in 2013,

Justine Sacco, 30 years old and the senior director of

corporate communications at IAC, began tweeting acerbic little jokes about the indignities of travel. There was one about a fellow passenger on the flight from John F. Kennedy International Airport:

"'Weird German Dude: You're in First Class. It's 2014. Get some deodorant.' Inner monologue as I inhale BO. Thank God for pharmaceuticals." Then, during her layover at Heathrow: "Chilly - cucumber sandwiches - bad teeth. Back in London!" And on Dec. 20, before the final leg of her trip to Cape Town:

"Going to Africa. Hope I don't get AIDS. Just kidding. I'm white!" She chuckled to herself as she pressed send on this last one, then wandered around

Heathrow's international terminal for half an hour, sporadically checking her phone. No one replied, which didn't surprise her. She had only 170 Twitter followers. Sacco boarded the plane. It was an 11-hour flight, so she slept. When the plane landed in Cape Town and was taxiing on the runway, she turned on her phone. Right away, she got a text from someone she hadn't spoken to since high school:

"I'm so sorry to see what's happening." Sacco looked at it, baffled. Then another text: "You need to call me immediately." It was from her best friend, Hannah. Then her phone exploded with more texts and alerts. And then it rang. It was Hannah. "You're the No. 1 worldwide trend on Twitter right now," she said. Sacco's Twitter feed had become a horror show.

"In light of @Justine-Sacco disgusting racist tweet, I'm donating to @care today" and "How did @JustineSacco get a PR job?! Her level of racist ignorance belongs on Fox News. #AIDS can affect anyone!" and "I'm an IAC employee and I don't want @JustineSacco doing any communications on our behalf ever again. Ever." And then one from her employer, IAC, the corporate owner of The Daily Beast, OKCupid and Vimeo: "This is an outrageous, offensive comment. Employee in question currently unreachable on an int'l flight."

The anger soon turned to excitement: "All I want for Christmas is to see @JustineSacco's face when her plane lands and she checks her inbox/voicemail" and "Oh man, @JustineSacco is going to have the most painful phone-turning- on moment ever when her plane lands" and "We are about to watch this @JustineSacco bitch get fired. In REAL time. Before she even KNOWS she's getting fired."

The furor over Sacco's tweet had become not just an ideological crusade against her perceived bigotry but also a form of idle entertainment. Her complete ignorance of her predicament for those 11 hours lent the episode both dramatic irony and a pleasing narrative arc.

As Sacco's flight traversed the length of Africa, a hashtag began to trend worldwide: #HasJustineLandedYet. "Seriously. I just want to go home to go to bed, but everyone at the bar is SO into #HasJustineLandedYet. Can't look away. Can't leave" and "Right, is there no one in Cape Town going to the airport to tweet her arrival? Come on, Twitter! I'd like pictures #HasJustineLandedYet."

A Twitter user did indeed go to the airport to tweet her arrival. He took her photograph and posted it online. "Yup," he wrote, "@JustineSacco HAS in fact landed at Cape Town International. She's decided to wear sunnies as a disguise." By the time Sacco had touched down, tens of thousands of angry tweets had been sent in response to her joke. Hannah, meanwhile, frantically deleted her friend's tweet and her account - Sacco didn't want to look - but it was far too late. "Sorry @JustineSacco," wrote one Twitter user, "your tweet lives on forever."[33]

Above is just a taste of what damage Twitter can do when careless. And with over 300 million users, there is bound to be some carelessness. On the other hand, it offers businesses and people in the public eye a quick way of reaching their customer (fan) base. Unfortunately - whenever high profile personalities deliver messages to that base, Twitter doesn't offer a filter on what *"should"* be said versus what *"is"* said. Public relations firms serve this purpose, often times providing damage control long after a tweet has surfaced and been deleted. Love it or hate it - it's here to stay.

Consequently, however, employers will certainly check to see if you have used it; plus - investigate whether any questionable tweets are lingering - causing an employer to shy away from hiring you in the event some are found. Thus - my reasoning for throwing caution into the wind for using it. As a general rule, my advice for current users is as follows.

If ever in a situation warranting a "reactionary"

response, due to an antagonistic tweet, *sleep* on it for 24 hours before pressing the "send" button. Let "cooler heads prevail." In this way, you will have had time to calm down, allowing for a clearer frame of mind. This before sending out an "*ill-advised*" tweet that could end up pouring gasoline onto the fire, causing damage to your reputation, and potentially your employer as well. Lastly, always "re-check" the *text* of your tweet to ensure the message you're about to send is intended.

Twitter isn't the only platform online that could cost a candidate a job. "Blogging" can be just as detrimental, especially after a background check reveals an affiliation with a controversial blog. And similar to Twitter, posting questionable content, regardless of nature, can land you on the outside looking in. Below is a story about a beer blogger I met who found this out the hard way while; uh, you guessed it; while out drinking beer!

The Beer Blogging Candidate:

I recently met a nice couple from the UK who asked what I did for a living, which led to some interesting interview stories after expressing I was in the process of writing this book. In particular, he shared how he was managing a beer blog and recently was interviewed for a marketing position. He added, the managers interrogating him asked point blank if he had a drinking problem. Whoa!

Though, I admit that's a pretty *bold* question, it didn't surprise me in the slightest, after hearing the words exit his mouth. Once more, he mentioned he was completely caught off guard and became defensive in the process. Can one blame him? After all, the prospective company is basically accusing him of having a drinking problem without even getting to know him. Ah ha! Behold. Therein lies the problem with having an "online" *presence.*

After showing me the blog on his smartphone, I too began judging him in the same manner as the employer had had. Consequently, he didn't get the job, but learned a hard lesson on how his *private* life could impact his professional one. Unfortunately, incidents like this occur repeatedly in today's digital world due to *ignorance.* Don't get me wrong – blogging is definitely a useful tool, but one has to be aware of their "audience" when doing so.

Blogging is a great way for owners to keep their customers informed. Yet, candidates must be self-aware of blogs that could cause a stir among the hiring ranks. For

335

instance blogs about: weapons; training pit-bulls for dog fighting; blogging about various types of cannabis; or even about the study of witchcraft will definitly raise some eyebrows and could knock you out of the race.

I am merely trying to warn you about how particular interests (if discovered) could lead to controversy and keep you from getting the job. This sounds blatantly obvious for most, but for others who aren't aware, upon signing your application, employers will pry into your private life in search of clues about "who you are." This applies to what you post online and when.

Privacy is a thing of the past, so with respect to social media, one must be mindful of not only the content they post, but also the location to where they post it. What's more, if you have an online presence, be aware of *inadvertent* information floating around that could be *damaging* to your reputation.

Keeping close tabs on what you say and "how" is key. This includes all content produced through personal blogs, YouTube, reviews, and comments-to- articles; because all of them could be viewed by the public through the "sharing" of unknown affiliates.

Safeguard it by all means necessary; including gaining control over your content, by conducting a Google search for damning text, which may or may not exist in order to remove it. Otherwise, you could be permanently black-balled throughout the corporate world, through no fault of your own.

This can occur with a seemingly harmless Facebook post from a friend - where you have been "tagged" in a photo (or video) that some may find offensive. If a potential employer were to discover this during a background check, it's conceivable they could judge you in a way – totally out of character – deeming you unfit for the job. If that scenario were to happen, it's likely the employer would never provide you the reason as to why they didn't hire you.

Ultimately – you would receive what I call the: "slap in the face" correspondence by your recruiter: *"The company has decided to move a step in a different direction."* In other words – "Thank you for showing interest in our company, but we have no reason to hire you." After working so hard to get the position and to lose it over one social media post would be tragic. Next up – should you *link-up* with "LinkedIn"?

LinkedIn:

LinkedIn originated from an idea between old colleagues "linked" together from SocialNet and PayPal, which has grown into a global icon. LinkedIn is now publically traded on the New York Stock Exchange (NYSE) with office locations worldwide. Few job seekers in this day and age can do without it. Reasons for using it.

For one thing, it's a great way to *network* in a world today where networking reigns supreme. Besides, it's just smart strategy, professionally, having a LinkedIn profile as it increases one's *visibility* to headhunters; in search of like professionals based on wanted credentials. Conversely, it's a great tool for those with lengthy career experience to have one central location for sharing their professional information.

On the other hand – having no profile at all could raise some red flags within some recruitment agencies, possibly resulting in lost opportunities. Likewise - if you claim to be a leader in your field and have limited followers linked to your profile, it could be viewed as a false assertion resulting in having your credibility challenged.

Another reason for using it is due to its ability in screening "referrals" from company personnel. Many companies offer referral programs in an effort to simplify the hiring process, allowing employees to pocket some extra cash. In fact – *referrals* are the #1 criteria for hiring new employees, and most companies today are paying in excess of a $1000 to $2000 per head.

LinkedIn can also help bridge the gap in vetting these referrals, by providing hiring managers access to candidate information that will aid them in making informed decisions about hiring them. For example – within minutes – an employee referral could be screened as a "yay" or "nay" – permitting the hiring manager to conclude the *suitability* of (X) candidate. Productivity, in terms of screening new candidates, would likely improve as a result.

Moreover - it's also a great platform for doing search inquiries for pin- pointing candidates with precise skill-sets for "hard to fill" jobs. Therefore - if you have a skill set *unlike* any other, it would behoove you to create a profile and include that for recruiters to seek you out.

Theoretically, this could open up global opportunities in advancing your career. Aside from that, if you prefer to do the seeking yourself, you have the liberty of applying online with the push of a button, providing yet another useful reason "why" to have a profile. Plausible reasons for not having one.

You could be judged negatively if you lacked a host of *connections* within a job sector due to a change in careers. To say it another way, if you had worked in sales for the past 10 years and now are in teaching for the past 3 with minimal LinkedIn connections in the education field, this would undoubtedly raise some eyebrows. Therefore – a career change may be best supported by staying on the sidelines in the beginning, and not creating a profile, if indeed you will be judged on the number of connections linked to it.

Another challenge is dispelling the belief you are "actively seeking" work upon *updating* your profile. This is a common problem without a "clear-cut" solution. If you are linked to a bunch of co-workers and are consistently updating your profile with weekly accomplishments, your co-workers, and manager for that matter, may think you're in the market for another job. In spite of this - if you're not keeping your profile "up to date" – then it's possible you could be losing out on better job opportunities.

The ultimate question is whether it's necessary to be on LinkedIn at all. The positives far outweigh the negatives and most recruiting experts say, *"absolutely yes"*. For sure, LinkedIn isn't going anywhere and recruiters will continue to rely heavily on it. The choice is obviously up to you, but based on surveying multiple recruitment agencies, if you don't have a profile, the odds of getting an interview will be significantly reduced compared to candidates with them.

Final thoughts:

Considerable information has been presented for you to chew on, regarding this topic. Social media is a great *networking* tool and platform for marketing purposes, but it can be quite "damaging" to one's career if not used carefully. Therefore, exercise caution when posting comments in various chat forums that could be denoted as *"questionable"* to an employer. "When in doubt – leave it out!"

Stay off Twitter unless you're already using it, and if so, use credence to my suggestions above by filtering yourself accordingly. *Lock* down all of your social media account settings by not allowing the "public" to view your posts. Use restraint in starting or becoming a member of a blog that could raise eyebrows (recall – beer blogging candidate). Plus be cognizant of the content you post online. "Untag" yourself in all photographs or videos posted on social media implicating you in a negative light.

One additional note before we move on – now that you've received the go- ahead from the company that you're their guy (gal), it's time for you to go on offense and squeeze as much money as feasibly possible, before signing on that dotted line. The time for negotiating salary begins now. You've won the battle against all the other candidates, now it's time for the company to pay up.

Chapter 12

NEGOTIATING SALARY

Fact! The only way to truly increase salary "exponentially" is to leave an existing job for another. Current employers provide "merit" raises yearly amounting to anywhere from 1.5% to 10% maximum, up to 20% in "extreme" cases.

Standard average is 3%! You heard that right. That's ridiculous in and of itself. Therefore, upon getting the job offer, it would behoove one to negotiate the highest salary possible. Because there are no second chances once the contract is signed.

All the same – this final chapter completes the process in providing you every tool necessary for acquiring work and maximizing pay, before ever stepping foot in the door. Take credence to the principles you're about to learn, because they will work for you as they did for me. All it takes is a little practice.

First – what to say if the compensation question comes up during the first interview. For example: What are your salary expectations? The majority of time the online "application process" will have already *screened* for this, but if not, I would answer it this way:

√   "That's a great question, however my top priority right now is to find a suitable match for my skill sets enabling me to grow within an organization, therefore I would consider all viable offers."

This demonstrates confidence in your abilities to go *elsewhere* if the offer isn't what you feel you deserve. However – in the event they press you for an answer it's a good idea (beforehand) to have an idea of a salary range expectation based on the job sector you're applying for. So if you're applying for a position in sales and marketing and the salary range is between $40,000-$50,000; you can articulate it in this manner:

√   "Based on industry standards within this sector, I expect to be paid in the range of $40,000-$50,000."

Three (3) Tier System:

After being offered the job, now what? It's time to fight for what is *rightfully* yours. The key is to remain calm and decline the "first" offer, unless you're desperate for the position and need income in a big way to save you from financial ruin. On the other hand – by having made it this far, you have *proven* your "value" to the organization in having "sold" them on the idea of you.

Consequently – being paid a premium now warrants itself as no employer wants 2nd best! That said, it's reasonable to expect a 20% window for negotiating salary contained within a "3-tier-system": Entry-level; Mid-level; Senior-level; and anything above would fall into "Executive level" status – requiring an entirely *different* negotiation altogether based on previous performance.

Aim high:

Since you have already interviewed for the position, you should have a general idea of the pay level based on the industry. This can easily be had researching salary ranges on the internet of company market share leaders within specific job sectors. After acquiring a benchmark, by and large, companies can negotiate within that 20% window. Therefore - if you're fresh out of college and recently accepted an "entry-level" customer care position, this job will pay around $25,000 per year.

So you can expect a 20% window to be in the neighborhood of $22,500 to $27,500. A mid-level position would involve a higher pay range, with a senior position comprising even higher. Upon being asked what your salary expectation is, always state a higher number, because you can never bid higher if you were to offer services at a lower salary. There are no second chances here. That said, don't go overboard.

Be realistic:

Usually the company will have covered salary requirements as a screening parameter beforehand. So being "realistic" is prudent based on job type, hence a project management position will offer significantly more pay than a customer care agent. The key to getting "top" salary is to play the game of *reiterating* your "strengths" and by explaining the "value" you will bring (monetarily) to the company based on (documented) past performance.

In other words – "Sell yourself"! It can be done in a manner that is both a "win-win" for you and the company. By negotiating a higher salary, you can sell the fact it will "offset" the additional resources necessary by earning "future revenue" for the company. Consequently – the additional revenues will (theoretically) yield higher profits, making the both of you happy in the process. It is said that "a happy employee is a *productive* one." A few more tips before sharing a role-play example.

Whenever HR presents you with the initial offer, be gracious and "thank" them for it, as both parties have worked extremely diligently in meeting each others' demands. Afterwards - express the following to whomever made the offer:

√   "It's a "generous" offer and you need some time to "think things through" – because you don't make "hasty" decisions."

This will create a sense of urgency on the company side to close the deal as soon as possible given the fact they have already committed to hiring you. Now the ball is in your court! Simply ask if they will allow you 24 hours (or even longer) to accept the offer. This will certainly throw them off, by not accepting the offer straightaway. Based on this fact alone, HR will generally offer you more upon asking for it. One word of caution, however, I wouldn't drag out the negotiation for more than one day. Sleep on it, call the next day, ask for at least a 10-15% raise based on *"specific"* reasons on what you can do for the company and then wait for an answer. Majority of the time, the company will say they need to get back to you; which is generally a positive sign they'll (at least) meet you "half- way."

> ✦ Never share negative body language or an impolite tone of voice (over the phone) if you feel the offer is "too"low.

The bottom line is that even if the offer is low, the probability of negotiating anything above 20% will be highly *unlikely* within a "multi-national" company. The exception (of course) lies within family-owned businesses or small companies who can *warrant* a higher salary due to their flexibility. An example of a potential conversation would look like this:

M – Manager | C – Candidate

> M: "Hello Kevin, I'm calling because I have good news! We would like to extend an offer to you for the position of "territory sales representative" How does that sound?"

C: "That's terrific! I'm really excited as I've been waiting to hear back from you."

M: "That's great to here, ok, here are the details. We are 'prepared' to pay you $45,000 per year; paid bi-weekly; plus you will receive full benefits and a car allowance of $500 per month. I will FedEx a package to you and you should receive it by tomorrow afternoon." (Note: Anytime an HR manager uses the word "prepared". It's a sign they can always offer more.)

C: "That sounds great! I'm so excited about coming to work for you guys. I can't wait to get started. May I ask how long the offer is "contingent" for?" (Note: At this moment in time the manager will have some doubt as to you accepting the job "as-is.")

M: "The offer is good for 48 hours. Do you need some time to think about it?"

C: "Let me start by saying how thankful I am to have been offered this position and as a general rule, I never make a hasty decision, so if it's possible I'd like to "sleep on it" and get back to you tomorrow if that's OK? One more question – I'm just curious – is the salary set in stone or do you have any flexibility?"

A couple of "major" points here:

1st: By slipping that last phrase in before ending the conversation: "One more question, I'm just curious, but is the salary 'set in stone' or do you have any flexibility?" This catches the manager completely "off-guard." Because, in their mind the conversation has ended, and when you hit them with that last question, they're generally more "relaxed" and will give you an honest answer.

2nd: Using the word "flexible" instead of "negotiate" is a nice way of softening the blow when asking for more money. Upon using this tactic in the past, two responses often occurred:

A. "No. I'm sorry, but the offer is final."

B. "Yes, 'to some degree' – but the highest we can manage to pay you based on your experience is $50,000. Will that work for you?"

This has worked like a charm for me in the past. By simply asking whether or not they have any *flexibility* in salary, HR would often express to me the top dollar figure they could pay out. Wouldn't that make you happy getting $5,000 more added on top of your starting salary? Of course it would!

Another approach in the event the manager "hangs-up" before you *slip* the last question in about flexibility. Wait for the next day and then ask them the *same* question in the manner above, or simply ask for more money based on your previous work results like so:

Candidate:

"Hello again. Thank you for allowing me the time to think this through. While I'm excited about the offer, I'd like to know if the salary is negotiable?" Or, you can use: "Can you tell me if you have any "flexibility" on salary? The reason for asking is based on my previous work history and results. I believe I will have an immediate impact in the territory, but I'd be remiss if I didn't ask you for a higher salary. Would that be possible?"

Regardless of whether the former or latter example is

used, it's still *"negotiating"* salary. There has never been a situation in my career where using this didn't at least "open" up a dialogue for discussion. Most companies have the flexibility, and if they don't, many times they will tell you *upfront* salary is "not" negotiable. Sometimes they may be stretching the truth; unfortunately, the only way to call them out on it is by *refusing* the offer.

Refusing an offer "entirely" should only be done if you have another company seeking your services. I found myself in this very situation - interviewing with two companies at the same time and was told by one the salary was "non-negotiable." Afterwards – I refused their offer, but then received a call-back shortly thereafter offering me a higher salary.

Much to their chagrin – I rejected their second offer, having already accepted an offer from the other firm. Just to be clear, I would never have done so had I not been offered the other job, beforehand. Keep that in mind when negotiating salary. Let me share one more *important* piece of advice regarding recruiters.

Recruiters get paid "commission" and will often *sweeten* a candidate's offer by accepting a *lower* commission to close the "sale." There have been instances where I was offered a "sign-on" bonus and negotiated a higher amount before accepting the offer.

As a general rule, they have good working relationships within the companies they represent. Therefore, they will know the salary ranges and whether they're negotiable or not. Furthermore - it's much easier for them to go to *bat* for you, than for you to negotiate *directly* with HR. So use them wisely and be upfront if you feel it necessary to ask for an increase in salary before signing the contract. They will respect you more. They will also negotiate more willingly on your "behalf" in getting you that increase as it's in their best interest to do so as well.

In the long-run - you are both trying to accomplish the same goal in obtaining higher pay. Once you sign the offer, there is no turning back. So don't ever give up without fighting for what is "rightfully" yours. You have come all this way and have proven yourself superior by beating out all the other candidates. HR, nor the recruiter, will want to lose you over a few thousand bucks after proving to them you are their #1 guy (gal).

Negotiating a higher salary within that 20% range isn't

going to ruffle any feathers, so be confident in asking for it by using the "proven" principles above and "close" the deal! You will be glad you did, and HR will be glad to have you.

CONCLUSION

I think it's safe to say you can now answer the question: "20 years of school – now what?!?" And, "Why You?" Additionally – you now have a good working knowledge on how to create a CV (resume) that sells, plus how to generate a cover letter triggering software algorithms to be selected for an interview.

I described (in length) my two golden-rules on how to develop a connection with your interviewer through establishing "Rapport" and finding "Commonality"; plus the importance of keeping an "interview-journal." Conversely, you're now aware of the 4 - Phases of the interview process and armed with knowledge on how to best prepare, including distinctive ways in answering "follow-up" questions.

In Chapter 6 – I shared my unique methodology (Identify - Improve - Embrace) on how to construct a viable "weakness." We also spoke about the use of particular "strengths" one should use based on job type.

Chapter 7 took your interviewing skills to another dimension by introducing you to the S.T.A.R. technique; aiding you in conquering the "competency-based" (structured) interview with special emphasis in answering "behavioral- questions." Through use of this technique – you now have the framework for answering: "Tell me about a time where you had a problem and how you solved it."

The chapters to follow yielded the importance of asking the "money- question" in order to flush out objections as to why "not" you countered effectively via "why you." Next – we covered in explicit detail on how to successfully navigate your way through an "assessment center." This followed by "final hurdles" you will endure upon being offered the job.

Moreover - the importance of how one's credit status and social media affiliations could negatively impact your chances of becoming hired. Lastly, we provided a solid foundation on negotiating maximum salary with HR through real-life examples - besides offering up some re-usable text templates.

In closing – it's both an honor and a pleasure to truly be a part of my future reader's success in helping you obtain the best job you can in support of your career maturation. The principles in this book helped me secure work in 7- *different* job sectors spanning over 25 years.

Interviewing is not easy, but my goal here was to provide as much clarity as genuinely possible by uncovering every conceivable scenario and by offering you the best solution in conquering them. You are now my judges on whether I accomplished that or not. I thank you all for your support and wish you success in your journey.

ABOUT THE AUTHOR

Kevin Mark Eagle is a father and U.S. native of Charlotte, N.C.; where he lived most of his young adult life. After graduating with a B.A. in Economics at the University of North Carolina (Charlotte), he then moved to Charleston, SC to take on his first job in outside sales for the next two years before landing into pharmaceutical sales, ultimately calling Orlando, FL home for nearly 10 years, before relocating back to his birthplace.

This after a failed attempt day-trading the NYSE & NASDAQ during the (dot)COM era in 2001. It was during this time where Kevin discovered his passion for writing after being interviewed by Associated Press and them publishing the interview in nearly every major newspaper outlet nationwide. All based on an editorial about initial public offerings (IPO's) in the U.S. stock market. Ten years later and back in Charlotte, Kevin would go on to experience more successes than failures. But after being caught up in the "Great Recession" through a corporate downsizing, it was time for a change.

In 2011 he visited Prague, met a nice local (Andrea), and relocated there to help raise their beautiful boy named Liam. Though no longer together, Kevin remained in Prague to be an intricate part of his son's life. Due to a language barrier and given his corporate experience, he decided to pursue his love for writing by teaching foreigners business English and writing skills. After 6 years of doing so, he has transitioned now into a "career-coaching" role helping clients with professional interview skills and resume (CV) writing.

Kevin has successfully secured employment professionally in 7 different industries with top Fortune 100 companies including: American-Airlines, Astra-Zeneca, AT&T, General Electric, Grainger, and Otis Elevator; yielding exemplary sales results; including - top sales honors for market share, revenue, and a President's Club nomination for leading the U.S. in net deals. Whenever Kevin is not engaged in one of his writing projects or interview-workshops in the US and abroad, he can be found spending quality time with his Czech/American son - Liam.

Bibliography

Interrogation Techniques for Better Interviewing Part 2: Phrasing and Positioning. (2012, March 12). Retrieved August 15, 2017, from Quick Base: http://www.quickbase.com/blog/interrogation-techniques-for-better- interviewing-part-2-phrasing-and-positioning

Aamodt, M. P. (2010, October 20). Meeting of October 20, 2010 - Employer Use of Credit History as a Screening Tool. Retrieved August 15, 2017, from

U.S. Equal Employment Opportunity Commission:https://www.eeoc.gov/eeoc/meetings/10-20-10/aamodt.cfm

Birnbaum, P. (2013, October 29). *A Guide to Sabermetric Research.* Retrieved September 10, 2017, from Society for American Baseball Research: http://sabr.org/sabermetrics

Cameron, J. (Director). (1984). *The Terminator* [Motion Picture].

Casti, T. (2013, September 10). *Mashable Social Media.* Retrieved August 15, 2017, from Mashable: http://mashable.com/2013/09/10/twitter-fights/#tRTnQQN5jgq0

Clark, B. (Director). (1983). *A Christmas Story* [Motion Picture]. Coppola, F. F. (Director). (1972). *The Godfather* [Motion Picture].

Darabont, F. (Director). (1994). *The Shawshank Redemption* [Motion Picture]. International, D. D. (2010). *The STAR Concept.* Pittsburgh: Development

Dimensions International.

International, D. D. (2017, October 8). The S.T.A.R. Technique. Pittsburgh, PA, USA.

Kennedy, M. (2016, January 1). *Assessment-centre-exercises/group-exercise- tips-and-advice.* Retrieved August 15, 2017, from Assessment Centre HQ: https://www.assessmentcentrehq.com/assessment-centre-exercises/group- exercise-tips-and-advice/

Kolb, D. (2009, June 26). *How To Interview.* Retrieved August 15, 2017, from Department of Biostatics - Vanderbilt University:

http://biostat.mc.vanderbilt.edu/wiki/Main/HowToInterview

Lewis, M. (2003). Moneyball - The Art of Winning an Unfair Game. Berkeley:

W. W. Norton & Company.

M, A. (2010, January 12). *SB 1045 - Job Applicant Fairness Act | Oregon State Legislative Hearing.* Retrieved August 15, 2017, from You Tube:
https://www.youtube.com/watch?v=RypwgmjZXow&feature=related

McKay, A. (Director). (2015, December 23). *The Big Short* [Motion Picture]. Miller, B. (Director). (2011). *Moneyball* [Motion Picture].

Newport, F. (2014, November 10). *poll 179288.* Retrieved August 15, 2017, from gallup.com:
http://www.gallup.com/poll/179288/new-era-communication-americans.aspx

Nolan, C. (Director). (2008). *The Dark Knight* [Motion Picture].

Petroff, A. (2013, September 24). *money.cnn.com companies.*

Retrieved August 15, 2017, from cnn.com:
http://money.cnn.com/2013/09/24/news/companies/b
ofa-racial- discrimination/index.html

RONSON, J. (2015, February 12). *newyorktimes.com
magazine*. Retrieved August 15, 2017, from
newyorktimes.com:
https://www.nytimes.com/2015/02/15/magazine/how-
one-stupid-tweet- ruined-justine-saccos-life.html

Ross, G. (Director). (2012). *The Hunger Games* [Motion
Picture].

Shepherd, J. (1983, November 18). *IMDB*. Retrieved
September 9, 2017, from IMDB:
http://www.imdb.com/title/tt0085334/

Simon, J. M. (2010, September 10). *credit card news*.
Retrieved August 15, 2017, from creditcards.com:
http://www.creditcards.com/credit-card- news/state-
laws-limit-employee-credit-check-1282.php

Smosh.com, E. (. (2018, January 27). 6-controversial-
tweets-celebrities-they- immediately-regretted.

Spielberg, S. (Director). (1975). *Jaws* [Motion Picture].

St., S. S. (2018, January 29). America's Most Hated Companies. Zemeckis, R. (Director). (1994). *Forrest Gump* [Motion Pictur e].

Made in the USA
Columbia, SC
28 September 2022

68129629R00224